Irises

Pamela McGeorge & Alison Nicoll

Photographs by
Russell McGeorge

FIREFLY BOOKS

In developing this book, the authors and the photographer have drawn on the experience of many iris enthusiasts. In particular we wish to thank Eddie Johns, Adrian and Bronwyn Ballinger of O'Tara Birch Gardens for giving us the 'run' of their garden for photography during the flowering season, and for their hospitality and advice. Our special thanks also to Barbara and Brian Harris of Waimate Iris Gardens and to Gwenda Harris of Otepopo Nursery in Hampden in whose gardens we took many photographs. They willingly shared their love and knowledge of irises. Many others contributed to our efforts: Piki Carrol, Darlene Cook, Lesley Cox, Maria Fairburn, Frances Love and Isobel Simpson; our grateful thanks go to them, to the iris growers – too numerous to name – who gave us the freedom of their gardens, and to Ernie Davis, Ron Goudswaard, Graeme Grosvenor and Gwenda Harris who read parts of the manuscript. This book was a most enjoyable project and we remain in awe of the beauty and variety of the genus iris.

Pamela and Russell McGeorge & Alison Nicoll.

The following photos were not taken by Russell McGeorge: Pages: 7, 78, 82, Gil Hanly; 26, Tim Hawkins, courtesy *NZ Gardener*; 35 (top), 44, 70, 71, 73, 74, 81, Jack Hobbs; 31, 35 (bottom), 36, 47 (left), 66 (bottom), 67, 75, 76, 77, NZ Iris Society; 38, Rosemary Thodey; 24, 47 (right), 88, Alison Nicoll; 58, Graham Smith; 63, 64, Graeme Grosvenor.

Page 1: Tall Bearded 'Dream Lover'.
Page 2: Iris flowers and foliage fit well in a cottage garden.
Page 3: Bearded iris 'Gracchus'.

A FIREFLY BOOK

Published by Firefly Books Ltd. 2001

Copyright © 2001 Pamela McGeorge, Alison Nicoll & David Bateman Ltd

First Printing

Library of Congress Cataloging in Publication Data is available.

Canadian Cataloguing in Publication Data

McGeorge, Pamela, 1943-
    Irises

Includes index.

ISBN 1-55209-567-3 (bound) ISBN 1-55209-506-1 (pbk.)

1. Iris (Plant). I. McGeorge, Russell, 1943-. II. Title.

SB413.I8M33 2001 635.9'3438 C00-931750-3

Published in the United States in 2001 by Firefly Books (U.S.) Inc.
P.O. Box 1338, Ellicott Station, Buffalo, New York 14205

Published in Canada in 2001 by Firefly Books Ltd.
3680 Victoria Park Avenue, Willowdale, Ontario M2H 3K1

Visit our web site at www.fireflybooks.com

Cover design by Shelley Watson, Sublime Design
Book design by Errol McLeary
Typesetting by Jazz Graphics
Printed in Hong Kong by Colorcraft Ltd

Contents

Introduction

There was a time when I didn't like irises. But that was before I knew about the gorgeous Japanese beauties with their delicate flat petals; before I had seen clumps of dainty, deep purple Siberian irises reflected in water, and before I met Alison Nicoll and her husband David at their iris garden and nursery in Nelson, New Zealand.

There I stood, surrounded by fields of Tall Bearded irises in more color combinations than I'd ever imagined. I picked huge armfuls of them – truly flowers of the rainbow goddess – and knew that never again would I feel the same about this plant.

Most people are familiar with irises. Their form has been celebrated in art for centuries and their legendary color combinations make them a flower that begs to be noticed, whether it be a simple species found growing in the wild or an exotic, highly bred cultivar. There is a difference, though, between merely recognizing an iris growing in someone's garden and knowing the many different kinds of irises and how best to grow them.

Irises grow wild in the alpine areas of China at altitudes of more than 12,000 ft (4000 m); they survive unscathed in the frozen winter wastes of Siberia. They thrive in moist oak woodlands and alongside streams, in pine forests and salt marshes, on rooftops and sandy banks in the shade. They proliferate in swamps in the United States and they ramble wantonly in ancient Arab cemeteries around the Mediterranean.

Most are easy to cultivate once their particular requirements are understood. But beware of their enchantment: they are incurably seductive flowers to meddle with. Succumb once to their beauty and you're an addict for life.

Part of the spell lies in their incredible variety. Some flower in mid-winter, others in mid-summer; some like to grow in water, others need to be baked dry in summer. There are stately aristocratic blooms, haughty in their slender classic shape; there are great blowsy beauties, over-developed and brazen; there are some with such delicate, refined markings you wonder where nature found the skill to create them. And there are some, a very few, that make you cringe with their bizarre mix of colors.

Given the right conditions, it is often possible to grow many different types in one garden. And the garden need not be huge, for there are irises that thrive in containers. Imagine the joy of growing a true water-iris in your own miniature pool, or the pleasure of watching a Japanese iris go from bud to bloom in a container on the deck outside your living room. Many irisarians enjoy growing plants from seed for results are satisfyingly quick. Unlike daffodils, which take between five and seven years from seed to flower, most irises take only two years.

There is a fascination with this genus that has beguiled priests, princes and plant propagators for thousands of years. Hybridizers are still intent on developing the flower and the plant in all sorts of intriguing ways. Awards are given for the best irises in any year and the most sought-after of these commemorates W R Dykes, considered by some to be the greatest English authority on irises. An enthusiastic hybridizer himself, he was instrumental in fostering a keen interest in the development of the genus in the early years of the 20th century.

Opposite: Clumps of Tall Bearded irises make an excellent focal point in a garden scene.

Grown in a pot, Japanese irises can enjoy their own environment among other plants.

possible, and all definitions appear in the glossary.

The plants seen in most gardens are hybrids; what was new 10 years ago may have disappeared from the market today, though there are old favorites which turn up in nursery lists year after year. Many gardeners start by growing hybrids and gradually find themselves ensnared into seeking rarer species. If it's not possible to find the actual plants, seeds are usually available through membership in an iris society. (A lively exchange of both seeds and information flows backwards and forwards between many countries.) A list of nurseries and iris societies can be found in the appendix.

This book is for the home gardener who has been seduced by the beauty of the flower of the rainbow goddess, and who wants to learn more about the individual plants, about their history and how to grow them.

The Dykes Medal is awarded by the British Iris Society. It is interesting to follow the development of the flowers over time by looking at the irises that have been awarded the Dykes Medal. Schreiner's gardens, in Salem, Oregon, have a collection of these winners on display. Here can be seen every Dykes Medal winner from the first American winner in 1927 – 'San Francisco' [W. Mohr] – to the most recent in 1999 – 'Hello Darkness' [Schreiner].

The genus is complicated. Botanists have divided it into divisions and groups according to particular characteristics that distinguish the various members and help with their identification, as well as with an understanding of their requirements. As with any speciality, there is a jargon the knowledgeable use when discussing their interest/obsession that can be very confusing to the uninitiated. In this book, the more technical terms have been avoided where

Hardiness Zone Map

This map has been prepared to agree with a system of plant hardiness zones that have been accepted as an international standard and range from 1 to 11. It shows the minimum winter temperatures that can be expected on average in different regions.

In this book, where a zone number has been given, the number corresponds with a zone shown here. That number indicates the coldest areas in which the particular plant is likely to survive through an average winter.

Note that these are not necessarily the areas in which it will grow best. Because the zone number refers to the minimum temperatures, a plant given zone 7, for example, will obviously grow perfectly well in zone 8, but not in zone 6. Plants grown in a zone considerably higher than the zone with the minimum winter temperature in which they will survive might well grow but they are likely to behave differently. Note also that some readers may find the numbers a little conservative; we felt it best to err on the side of caution.

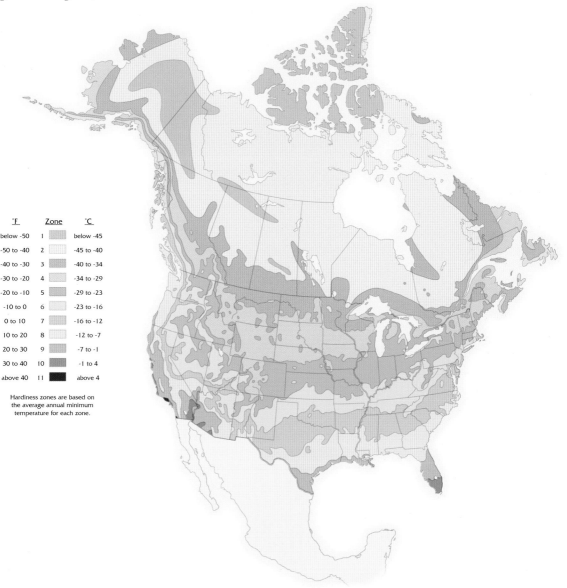

°F	Zone	°C
below -50	1	below -45
-50 to -40	2	-45 to -40
-40 to -30	3	-40 to -34
-30 to -20	4	-34 to -29
-20 to -10	5	-29 to -23
-10 to 0	6	-23 to -16
0 to 10	7	-16 to -12
10 to 20	8	-12 to -7
20 to 30	9	-7 to -1
30 to 40	10	-1 to 4
above 40	11	above 4

Hardiness zones are based on the average annual minimum temperature for each zone.

CHAPTER 1

History and Outline of the Genus

The iris is an aristocratic flower with connections that go right back in time. The earliest iris was probably cultivated as long ago as 7000 BC. Did you know the Egyptians used the iris to adorn statues of the sphinx? That it appeared on the scepters of their kings, its trinity of parts representing faith, wisdom and valor? That it appears carved on a hieroglyph in the burial chamber of an Egyptian king who lived 1500 years before Christ was born?

Almost as ancient is the confusion between lilies and irises. In the Bible we are asked to 'Consider the lilies . . .', but botanists claim that it would be more accurate to consider the irises for there are no lilies to be found in the Holy Land, whereas *Iris albicans* (beloved of the Arabs), *I. cypriana* and *I. madonna* used to grow wild there. And if we are to believe the New Testament writer, these flowers were considered even more magnificent than Solomon and all his glorious trappings of kingship. Iris lovers today would surely agree with this comparison!

Much later, Clovis, a warrior leader of the Franks in the 6th century, took *I. pseudacorus* as his kingly symbol, though his reasons vary according to which book you read. Mrs Grieve, in *A Modern Herbal*, claims he was facing defeat in battle and prayed to the god of his Christian wife, Clothilde, who heard his pleas for victory. In gratitude, Clovis duly turned Christian and replaced the three toads on his banner with three iris blooms, said to be the flower of the Virgin.

Opposite: *Iris setosa* and *Primula prolifera*.

But Alice M Coats in her *Flowers and their Histories* asserts that Clovis was caught between a rock and a hard place: at his back a superior force of barbarians, in front of him, the river Rhine. Not given to panic, Clovis noticed flag irises growing far out into the river, realized the water must be shallow enough to ford, and so led his army to safety. In recognition, he adopted the flower of the flag iris as his emblem.

Six centuries later, Louis VII revived the use of this royal emblem and used it on his banners when he went crusading. It took his name: Fleur de Louis, later corrupted to fleur-de-lis, or flower of the lily. Or was it that *I. pseudacorus* grew abundantly along the banks of the River Lys in France, the emblem becoming known as Fleur-de-Lys, also transcribing to Fleur-de-lis? The heraldic flower has been identified as undoubtedly that of *I. pseudacorus*, but to confuse the issue even further, it *may* have started life as Fleur-de-luce, flower of light, referring to the golden color of the iris. Lilies it seemed were never in the picture!

The form of the iris, no less than its glorious colors, has been beloved by artists for centuries. Look at the paintings of Old Masters and you will find irises among their floral compositions. Painters in Italy and Holland included irises in their religious pictures as a symbol of the royal birth of Christ – an interesting liberty surely when you consider its use as a royal emblem was often to invoke success in battle! It appears in ancient embroideries of Persia, China and Japan. In India the Taj Mahal has the iconic *I. susiana* carved into its stone.

Iris laevigata 'Alba', primulas and astilbe.

Irises also have a long history as plants with medicinal uses and commercial value in perfumery. In Greek times, the philosopher Theophrastus described what is probably *I. pallida* and made reference to its rhizome, valued for the perfume it produced. Gerard, in his famous herbal, refers to the iris as 'Floure-de-luce' and claims it has the power to take away bruises. In Mrs Grieve's herbal she lists other virtues attributed to irises – the ability to remove freckles, effectiveness in treatment of bronchitis, of chronic diarrhea, dropsy, and obstinate coughs. The dried powder of the root was used as snuff and in Italy the dried rhizome was given to toddlers to chew on to relieve the pain of teething.

I. florentina, *I. pallida* and *I. germanica* were at one time widely cultivated in Tuscany, Italy. Three-year-old rhizomes were harvested annually, dried, and then exported to England as orrisroot, precious for the violet-like perfume exuded from the rhizomes once they were powdered. A flourishing industry in the 19th and early 20th centuries, it faded with the manufacture of synthetic fragrances. Interestingly, the Romans flavored their wine with orrisroot.

I. foetidissima in the past was used to produce a dye, yellow from the flowers, black from the roots. *I. tenax* was valued by North American Indians for the strength of its leaf fiber from which they used to weave twine or cord.

Iris genus

Irises belong to the family Iridaceae which includes freesias and gladioli, plants that, to the casual observer, have nothing in common with the iris. The family also includes plants that look very much like irises, yet are classified under other names. Such plants are Moraea from South Africa, Tigridia from South America, and Dietes, a real iris lookalike, also from South Africa. But no true iris is native to the southern hemisphere.

Diagram 1: Characteristics of iris flower using bearded iris as the example.

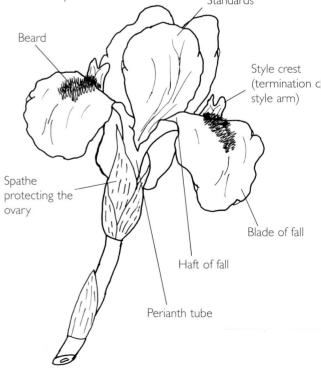

Standards

Beard

Style crest
(termination c
style arm)

Spathe
protecting the
ovary

Blade of fall

Haft of fall

Perianth tube

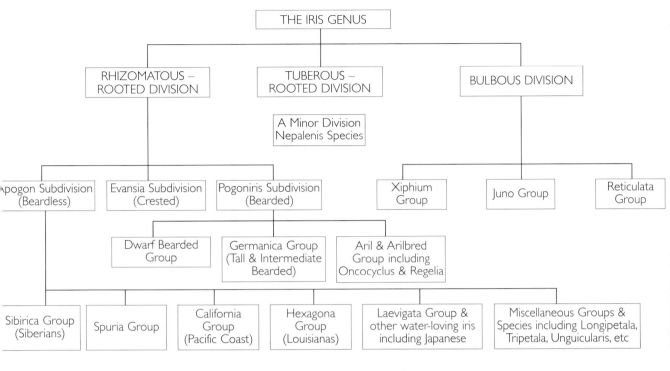

Simplified Diagrammatic Key
To The Iris Genus

Widely dispersed across Europe, Asia and parts of North America, irises are recognizable by the arrangement of their floral parts in multiples of three. They have six floral segments (or petals) in two sets – the standards and the falls. Standards are named for their tendency to sit upright; falls tend to droop and are often broader than the standards. These parts are merely the decoration, and have no role to play in the reproduction of the plant.

As well as the falls and standards, irises have three style arms that are evident when you look down on the bloom. These radiate from the center of the bloom, overlaying the falls and adding to the beauty of the flower with their distinctive colors. But they have a specific purpose: they are extensions of the ovaries, which contain the egg cells. Once pollinated, the ovary swells to become the seed pod and in some cases this can be enormous, as the photograph of a seedling Louisiana seed pod on page 62 demonstrates. Styles, ovaries, stigmas and anthers all constitute the sexual or seed-forming parts of the iris.

Bewitching to look at, the often surreal color combinations created by the different parts of the flower are not produced merely for humans to marvel at, though they play a large part in making us fall in love with the plant. The iris is flaunting its beauty to attract pollinating insects. This attraction is enhanced by a feature on the falls, a landing strip that tempts the insect closer and says, "Hey, stop a minute and see what I have to offer!" In the case of bearded irises, it is the beard. On beardless varieties it may be a bold bright signal, a stripe in a contrasting color or a frilled crest. Stand for a few moments one warm sunny day when the irises are in flower and watch a bumblebee head straight for the narrow slot created by the style arms spreading over this patch at the top of the falls. The bee disappears as if through a secret trapdoor, greedy for the nectar found at the base of the flower, and in the process fertilizes the plant.

The genus consists of more than 200 species, many of which have hybridized naturally in the wild, cross-pollinated by insects. This sometimes makes it difficult, when "new" finds have been made, for botanists to distinguish between true species (i.e. a plant having characteristics it does not share with any other plant in the same genus), and natural hybrids. Classification still continues and as new genetic information comes to light, name changes occur from time to time.

As hybridizers work their magic – breeding new cultivars – the most visible effects of their alchemy are increasing color ranges in particular series, and flowers that have changed in shape from the species. In many cases, the falls have become broader and, especially in the case of Japanese irises, more horizontal. Standards often have become less upright.

Substance is the term used to refer to the thickness of the floral parts: the more substantial the petals, the longer the flower tends to last, either on the plant or as a cut flower, and the better is its resistance to heat, rain and wind. But where fragility is part of the charm of a particular flower, increased substance may not necessarily be regarded as an improvement.

Texture refers to the surface of the floral parts; they may be velvety or silken, glossy or mat, smooth or papery.

With the advent of the chemical breeding of tetraploids (plants with cells that contain four sets of chromosomes instead of the usual two), and the crossing of natural tetraploids (in the case of bearded irises), hybridizers started creating flowers which are larger, more ruffled, more flaring in form, and richer in color, while various features of the plant are emphasized. The leaves and stalks are frequently thicker and a deeper green, the substance of the petals or their velvety texture may be exaggerated.

These three flowers show the evolution of a Japanese bloom. First cross from a species, this bloom still exhibits the classic shape with pendent falls.

Not everyone, however, applauds these changes. Irisarians can be passionate about their favorite flowers. Those who love the simplicity of the species are often vociferous in their defence, deploring a radical departure from their basic form.

Hybridizers also look to increase the all-around garden performance of irises, to create plants that are healthier and more floriferous, that will produce more branches, that will bloom more than once in a season (remontancy), or that will tolerate a wider range of climate differential. And the search is on to create a truly red iris though there are now some Louisianas that come close.

Root structure

Just as the flowers of different irises vary, so do the structures that support them beneath the ground.

An iris may grow from a bulb (a modified collection of leaves that stores food for the plant), from tubers, or from rhizomes, which store nutrients and resemble somewhat chunky fingers, themselves producing roots in the growing season to anchor the

'Good Omen', a six-petaled hybrid.

An unnamed, hybrid, nine-petaled seedling is an example of the multi-petaled or peony form.

Diagram 2: Root structures

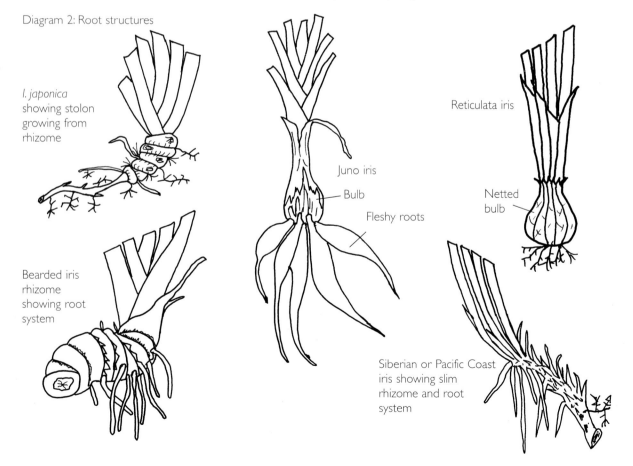

I. japonica showing stolon growing from rhizome

Bearded iris rhizome showing root system

Juno iris

— Bulb

Fleshy roots

Reticulata iris

Netted bulb

Siberian or Pacific Coast iris showing slim rhizome and root system

plant in the ground. The rhizomes of bearded irises are thick, those of Siberian irises are thinner, but both kinds reproduce by annual increase of rhizomes as well as by producing seeds.

Rhizomes of *I. japonica* and *I. confusa*, members of the Evansia, or Crested, clan of irises, increase by stolons that creep underground and produce a fan of leaves at their tip.

Foliage

Most gardeners choose irises for their stunning color or for their classic form. But as members of a community of plants, foliage and behavior throughout the seasons become important design factors. After all, the foliage will still be there, irritating or satisfying, long after the blooms have faded, and all irises have foliage that defines the shape of the plant.

Foliage of the tiny spring-flowering Reticulatas can be less than appealing once the flowers have gone, but the leaves need to remain on the plant to replenish its resources for the following season. So it's a good idea to plant these early-flowering irises where their foliage will be hidden by the new growth of later developing spring plants.

Dwarf Bearded irises also flower early in spring, but in contrast to Reticulatas their foliage is still handsome in mid-summer, providing fans of upright light green blades – an attractive focus in the front of the border among low, sprawling perennials.

Siberian irises, on the other hand, form tall graceful fountains of fine grass-like foliage that in themselves become a garden feature until they die down in the fall. So, once seduced by the flower of a particular iris, it's a good idea to consider carefully where it will look best.

Culture

Soils vary considerably in their composition, from extreme acidity to extreme alkalinity, the relative measure being expressed as the pH value; 7 is neutral. A pH reading of 6.5 and lower indicates soil of acidic composition with the level of acidity

increasing as the number decreases. A reading above 7 indicates that the soil is alkaline, and the higher the number, the higher the alkalinity. Some irises like soil that is alkaline in its composition; many require an acidic soil. Providing the right soil for the kinds of iris you want to grow is very important. So too is the amount of moisture that is required. Think about where the iris grows naturally and then try to simulate those conditions as closely as possible. Obviously, if you garden at sea level you cannot do much to increase the altitude but, depending on

Siberian 'Caesar's Brother' planted *en masse*.

what your favorite iris requires, you can ensure that the ground is boggy or well-drained or somewhere in between. And you can add nutrients to the soil to adjust its chemical composition. Agricultural sulfur, rotted animal manure, pine needles and leaf mold all help to maintain the acidity of the soil. Treating it with lime or dolomite will increase its alkalinity.

Remember also that the climate you garden in will affect flowering times. Bearded irises, for example, grown in zone 9, may flower up to a month earlier than bearded irises grown in the colder zone 8.

In the following chapters zone information for species and cultivars is provided as an indication only. Hardiness depends on a great many factors. For example, often it is excessive moisture rather than the cold that will kill irises. Where a range of zones is given for an iris group, generally species and hybrids will grow within this range. If, however, this is not the case, a specific zone will be given with the species or cultivar under its main entry.

CHAPTER 2

Bearded Irises

Bearded irises are probably the most widely recognized of all iris flowers and most of us no doubt remember them growing in our parents' or grandparents' gardens. Their often striking color combinations ensure that these are not flowers to forget in a hurry. Each spring, the magnificent sight of massed plantings or individual blooms inspire artists and photographers to take their paints or grab their cameras and rush out to record this impressive plant in flower.

Visitors "ooh" and "aah" with delight when they visit our iris beds, where we grow large numbers of irises for sale. The beds are situated in an orchard where the fresh green foliage of old plum and pear trees provides a perfect background for the annual riot of color. If there are any commercial fields near you it is well worth the trip to feast your eyes on the breathtaking display these flowers make *en masse*.

Plant characteristics

Bearded irises are stately plants. Tall or small they produce flowers of elegant form. They grow from a rhizome with fans of sculptured, sword-shaped, bluish green leaves standing stiffly upright or curving gracefully at their tips. In some varieties the leaves have a surprising and attractive purplish red tinge at the base. The waxy coated leaves express the overall well-being of the plant, with healthy leaves having a bluish tinge and growing vigorously from the middle of each fan.

Opposite: Tall Bearded 'Epicenter'

Tall Bearded 'Cabaret Royale'

The rhizome, or swollen stem, is where the plant stores nutrients and moisture, enabling it to survive a certain amount of stress. Spring growth occurs immediately after flowering, usually for about one or two months. During mid-summer the plants take a rest, with further growth occurring again in the fall before the leaves die down and the plant enters a dormant state for winter.

Rhizomes grow along the surface of the soil, sending leaf fans upwards and roots downwards from their growing end. During the heat of summer the rhizomes become hardened, protecting the resources within and making it difficult for pests and diseases to gain entry. However, long periods of wet

19

Tall Bearded 'Copatonic'

Tall Bearded 'Helene C'

weather can soften and weaken the rhizome, allowing slugs or other pests a hearty meal.

Rhizomes naturally divide and increase annually, eventually forming a complex interwoven mat. To ensure good flowering each season, the plant should be divided before this stage. Each rhizome will flower only once and then grow new rhizomes behind the current season's flower stem, or sometimes from buds along the rhizome's length. Multiplying in this way gives the plant the opportunity to access further nutrients in newer soil. The fan itself is the leading edge of the growth point and from here the plant marches outwards, away from the spent mother rhizome. Different varieties increase and grow at varying speeds, some producing a large number of increases each year, others comparatively few.

Flower characteristics

As with all irises, the flower consists of three standards, three falls and three style arms. In the bearded irises, the delicately dome-shaped standards usually close over the top of the flower protecting the style arms, which are often beautifully colored. The stigmatic lip or female part of the flower lies on their underside; the pollen-bearing anther, or male part of the flower, hides directly under the stigmatic lip.

Curving outwards and downwards, the falls or lower petals display the beard, an appendage somewhat like a large fuzzy caterpillar, which is the main distinguishing characteristic of this group.

Beards come in many colors, even the same color as the flower, giving an intense overall effect. The heavily ruffled purple-black 'Night Ruler' (Schreiner 1990), is a good example. Beards may also be a completely different color as seen in 'Stately Art' (Aitken 1997), where the lovely blue is complemented by a surprisingly red beard.

Left: 'Bewilderbeast', a new hybrid Tall Bearded from Elwood, Utah.

Beards add character and charm to the flower, enhancing and complementing the colors in the falls. In some hybrids the beards may also have extensions or horns and other interesting appendages such as spoons and flounces. The white iris 'Mesmerizer' (Byers 1991), with its frilly flounces, has an appearance of a double flower. 'Thornbird' (Byers 1989), an unusual tan, has remarkable bright violet horns. Irises with these characteristics are known as "Space Age" irises.

Falls may be frilled, smooth or ruffled, broad or narrow, and may stand out like a saucer, fall gently downwards or recurve under the flower. (This last is a characteristic of Oncocyclus irises.)

The flowers of bearded irises, once open, will remain in good condition for about three days, depending on the temperature. It is simple to remove spent flowers as they close. Supporting the base of the new bud firmly, carefully bend the spent flower down and out with a sharp movement. It should snap cleanly away from the socket.

Color patterns vary widely from single to multiple hues that include streaking, thumbprints and veining. There are special names to denote particular patterns. A single color, for example, is known as a "self" and Schreiner's 1990 release of 'Blenheim Royal' is a fine example of a true, rich, purple self. A "plicata" has stippling, stitching or dotting on the outer margin of the petals, particularly the falls, which contrasts with the lighter background color. A good example of a plicata is Schreiner's 'Rare Treat' (1987), a purple-on-white plicata. Other patterns are detailed in the glossary.

The flower spike of Tall Bearded irises should have at least two branches with both stem and branches producing several flowers. Ideally a good spike will have strong branches curving out from the main stem and supporting the flowers in a balanced and upright manner, not unlike a candelabra. Perfection is three flowers open at once in a balanced form, evenly spaced down the spike.

Tall Bearded 'Mesmerizer', one of the new "Space Age" bearded irises.

A recent Tall Bearded hybrid, 'Thornbird'.

The Dwarf Bearded irises are known for their thumbprints of rich contrasting color below the beard, a pattern that is only just beginning to emerge in the Tall Beardeds.

Climate

Most temperate climates are well-suited to growing these lovely flowers (zones 7-10). The ideal is a warm dry summer, followed by fall rains, a cool winter and a warm moist early spring. However, all bearded irises will tolerate variations. Recently it

Tall Bearded 'Just for You'

Spring and fall rains coincide with the root growth of the plant, helping the rhizome to store nutrients and moisture for use in times of scarcity.

A dry summer coincides with the semi-dormancy of the plant. Little growth occurs at this time but most leaves remain strong and firmly attached to the plant. Those that detach soon shrivel and fall, papery dry at the base of the fan. The rhizome hardens and bakes in the hot sun; in very hot climates it may even suffer from sunburn. This hot dry spell, complemented with a cool winter chill, perhaps contributes to the initiation of next season's flower spikes.

Summer rain and high humidity are not favored by bearded irises. The sword-shaped leaves are designed to direct moisture down to the soil close to the plant. If rain is followed by very hot sun, any water trapped in the leaves may boil, literally cooking the leaf base. I have seen this happen with water trapped in the bracts where flowering branches emerge. The result was collapsed branches! Damage such as this may allow bacteria and fungal spores to get in. Long periods of warm rain also encourage the development of fungal and bacterial leaf spot and rhizome soft rot, and in areas where summer rainfall is high it can become difficult, even with raised beds, to grow and increase bearded irises successfully.

rained for us every day the Tall Beardeds were in flower and they still looked magnificent. Large numbers of people carrying umbrellas and wearing rubber boots flocked to view the display.

Severe, long winters with snow and frosts can damage the plants. Frosts heave the rhizome out of the ground. But don't despair – standing on them firmly presses them back in. However, occasional frosts or cold snaps are not usually a problem and cold winters are beneficial in cleaning up any soil-borne diseases, reducing fungal spores and also hardening the rhizomes.

The most obvious cold damage happens when a late frost or snowfall occurs during the flowering period. This is when the flowers are tender and they can be ruined overnight. The buds, with luck, will survive this indignity.

It is quite an unusual sight to see irises, in all their beauty, standing in a carpet of snow – but upsetting if they have been totally spoiled! I have seen irises with snow on the ground at flowering time. Some blooms were ruined, but the following day warm sun brought out fresh flowers that looked quite lovely. Visitors to the 1998 American Iris Society convention in Denver had a similar experience.

Tall Bearded 'Tempting Fate'

Culture

Bearded irises are plants that thrive in sun. Choose an open area, making sure that sunlight is freely available for at least half the day. Avoid over-shadowing by trees and if you choose a site at the edge of a shrubbery, ensure that the shrubs are trimmed back each season so they do not overgrow the irises. They like free-draining, rich, neutral to alkaline soil, and if the area tends to be wet, the bed will need to be raised to avoid waterlogging. Bearded irises do not like clay or soil that is acidic in content. They are heavy feeders, doing best in soils that have a high humus content.

When preparing a new bed, incorporate compost and general garden fertilizer dug in well below the rhizome. Avoid fresh, strong manures as these can burn the rhizome and excessive nitrogen will cause a flush of soft fresh growth, softening the rhizome and providing ideal conditions for rhizome soft rot. A suitable fertilizer is 7-7-7 at $3^1/_2$ oz per square yard (100 gm per square meter). Scatter the fertilizer on the ground and work it in during digging in the early spring, about the time that crocus are in flower. A light dusting with fall rains is also beneficial.

The most important ingredient is humus which, after three years, will be almost depleted. Transplant the irises to a new area and the results can be

Tall Bearded irises look their best planted in groups.

dramatic, with a finger-thick rhizome swelling to a fat sausage size within weeks of the new roots taking hold.

Division

After two or three years, the older rhizomes at the center of a clump become unproductive. To maintain its vigor, the plant needs to be divided and transplanted. The best time is after flowering, when the fleshy white roots visible under the leaf fan easily identify the growth period. Divided then, the plant will quickly re-establish itself, securing the rhizome firmly in the ground and enabling it to support the next tall flower stem without toppling over.

Transplanting during periods of dormancy, such as in winter, is not a good idea as the plant will have to survive on the stored resources of the rhizome. As the next period of growth is not until after flowering, it is likely that the flower stems will be shorter, and flowers smaller than normal.

To divide an existing clump, first dig up the whole plant using a strong garden fork. Keep only

'Owyhee Desert', a new hybrid Tall Bearded from Parma, Idaho.

Left: Tall Bearded rhizome in growth, exposed to show the ideal planting depth. Center: Tall Bearded rhizome after two years, showing the increase of four new rhizomes. Right: By year three, it is ready for dividing.

the best new plump rhizomes with fresh, strong, green leaf fans and good root systems. Separate them from the older plant with a clean cut. They should be no shorter than the length of a thumb. Trim the leaves by about one-third. This helps prevent both wind-rock and excessive moisture loss while the new roots establish themselves. Discard the older unproductive rhizomes – they can be composted. Trimming the roots is a matter of preference, and I prefer not to, leaving sufficient to secure the plant firmly in the ground.

Planting

Plants purchased from an iris nursery will arrive by mail or courier and the roots will be bare. Check the plants for firm rhizomes and dry leaves. Don't panic if the leaves tend to be dry and browning; this is how they ought to be. There should be strong roots, which may have been evenly trimmed, but they should still be at least 4-6 in (10-15 cm) long. Allow free exposure to the air and keep them in a cool, dry place while you prepare the bed. To remember their names, garden labels cut from old venetian blind slats work well, and if you write with a 6B pencil it will not fade as some markers do.

Plant the rhizome with its top level with the soil surface. Having prepared the soil, dig a hole wide enough to take the young rhizome with outspread

roots. Place it in the center of the hole on a raised hump of soil, carefully spreading the roots downwards and away from the rhizome, deep enough to secure the plant firmly. I always treat these first roots as anchors to secure the plant, which will soon grow its own new feeder roots. Wind-rock or movement is the worst enemy of newly planted bearded irises as the new roots can be rubbed off as soon as they emerge. Fill in around the plant with the removed soil and press firmly with your foot. Check that the

Standard Dwarf Bearded iris as it comes from a nursery, ready for planting.

rhizome is level with, or above the natural level of, the soil. Water generously after planting and thereafter keep the soil slightly damp for about two weeks. Once the new roots appear, the plant will be able to withstand dry periods.

For group plantings per square yard (per square meter) allow three Tall Bearded rhizomes and four Intermediates and Borders. For Miniature, Standard Dwarf and Miniature Tall Bearded varieties, allow five or six double rhizomes.

Hygiene

During the growing season, the rhizome grows along the ground with the fan of leaves and new roots leading the way. New leaves come up in the center of the fan and the older leaves get pushed to the outside, eventually browning, falling and covering the rhizome. In very hot climates these decaying leaves may protect it from sunburn, but beware: in more temperate climates the spent leaves can provide cover for slugs, snails, slaters and earwigs, as well as host spores of fungal diseases. It is wise to check the plants frequently during the summer, removing all older foliage. Leaves are the source of many nutrients for the plant and to ensure a good season to follow, leave as much foliage as possible during the growing period.

It is essential to keep the clump weed-free and not allow overgrowth by other plants. Bearded irises are not hard to keep clean, so long as you understand their growth habit. Removal of large weeds with tap roots, such as dock or dandelion, can be achieved quite easily by using a sharp spade. A single deep angular plunge beneath the rhizomes (not directly in front of or close to the leaf fans) will cut the tap root of the offending weed. Place your foot firmly on the rhizomes and pull the weed out. It should come easily without the clump suffering any ill effects. Roots tend to be widespread and shallow, and with only one spade cut, very few will be damaged.

Quack grass, also known as twitch grass, can be a

Tall Bearded 'Adobe Rose'

real nuisance; it is best to remove the plants during times of growth, then spray the grass with a selective herbicide and ensure the area is clean before replanting. If the grass is very lush and green, it may be possible to wipe the leaf with a wand without also killing the iris but there is some risk in doing this.

Types of Bearded iris

Bearded irises are divided into categories determined by their height with the total flowering period lasting from 8-12 weeks and the flowering sequence generally going from smallest to tallest. The parade starts with the Dwarf Beardeds, usually March in warmer zones. But this will vary from zone to zone, with later flowering times in colder areas. Remember they all increase in size by growing new rhizomes each season. The small plant you start out with will double its size each year. What you can grow will be dictated by the size of your garden and climatic conditions.

Miniature Dwarf Bearded

44 in (20 cm) and under

These delightful, tiny, early spring-flowering irises are great for small gardens. They are ideal in a rockery, for the vigorous root systems search out moisture under the rocks and help to secure the plant. Or plant them at the edge of a sunny border in a frost-free site where they compensate for their small size with a cheerful multitude of flowers. But take care that they are not overgrown or over-shadowed by other plants.

By the second year a single rhizome will form a circular clump, giving a good display of bloom. Grow these little gems in containers in a courtyard, keep them sheltered while they are flowering and enjoy their gorgeous colors.

If your area is prone to late frosts and you can't find a protected site, it might be wise to settle for the Standard Dwarfs, which bloom later and are not so much at risk. Recommended varieties include: 'Linc' (Love 1973), lemon self; 'Surprise Orange' (Collins 1974), bright yellow orange; and 'Mini Plic' (Brown 1968), white stitched violet.

Standard Dwarf Bearded

44-54 in (20-38 cm)

Slightly taller than the Miniature Dwarfs, these come in a vast array of color combinations, many with interesting patterns and thumbprints on the falls. Flowers should stand above the foliage and multiple blooms may in fact hide the leaves altogether when they are in full flower. Often the rhizome sends up several stems, adding to the number of flowers and, with several buds on each stem, they offer an extended flowering season.

Tuck these plants into containers as growth begins and you'll have a burst of color ready to move into a prominent place in your garden when they flower. But put them back in the garden when flowering is over, as that is when they increase rapidly and quickly form a large clump.

A wide choice of varieties is available, including:

A brilliant early spring display of Dwarf Bearded irises and dwarf phlox.

'Babe' (Gatty 1981), a purple-on-white plicata; 'Celcius' (Blyth, 1985), lemon with red-brown signal; 'Chanted' (Blyth 1990), smoky pink; 'Chubby Cheeks' (Black 1984), ruffled light blue plicata; 'Cimmaron Rose' (Nichols 1990), blended rose red standards.

Intermediate Bearded

84-176 in (38-80 cm)

These are prolific bloomers and the flowers are great

Opposite: Intermediate Bearded 'Protocol'

for picking – not too big for the sideboard or table. Withstanding more wind than the Tall Beardeds, they flower after the Standard Dwarfs and usually before the Tall Beardeds. The branched stems produce multiple buds, helping to extend the bloom time. A great color range is available, and the plants are often vigorous and strong.

Recommended varieties are: 'Just Dance' (Blyth 1995), peach/buff/apricot; 'Furioso' (Blyth 1996), sweetly perfumed pinkish orange; 'Ingenious' (Blyth 1996), rosy violet; 'Min Min' (Catton 1990), mustard gold, vigorous; 'Wild Lad' (Blyth 1996), tan/apricot/buff with purple midriff infusion on standards and purple infusion on hafts of falls, bronze black beards; 'Wind Spirit' (Blyth 1996), mauve violet with vibrant tangerine beards.

Border Bearded
84-156 in (38-71 cm)

These flower at the same time as the Tall Beardeds and are lovely planted in front of them as they too are more tolerant of wind and less likely to be buffeted about. Although less well-known than the other types, a good range is available.

Recommended varieties include: 'Batik' (Esminger 1986), unusual streaked white on purple; 'Brown Lasso' (Buckles/Niswonger 1975), butterscotch standards and violet falls edged brown; 'Ingenious' (Blyth 1995), rosy violet standards, with ruby-black

Border Bearded 'Batik'

falls; 'Pink Bubbles' (Hagar 1980), ruffled and flared flamingo pink.

Miniature Tall Bearded
84-156 in (38-71 cm)

Miniature Tall Beardeds are superb miniature forms of the Tall Beardeds, with slim stems and dainty flowers – elegant plants, ideally suited to small suburban gardens. They have fine leaves and quite small rhizomes. The flowers are lovely for picking for a table or small arrangement. I find it's a good idea to mark where they are grown as they are easily lost in the border with other vigorous plants.

Favorites for me include: 'Proven Stock' (Fisher 1997), wheat-colored standards and plum-purple falls with a fine tan rim; 'New Idea' (Hagar

1970), rose-mulberry; 'Bettina' (Dunderman 1981), orchid-pink on white plicata; 'Carolyn Rose' (Dunderman 1970), stitched (dotted) rose pink on white. Sometimes included with these and ever-popular is a very old iris called 'Gracchus', bred in 1886, with lemon standards and a red pattern on the falls. It always looks fresh and lovely.

Tall Bearded

Over 176 in (80 cm)

The Tall Beardeds are majestic, bold, large and beautiful, and so flamboyant that to plant them *en masse* they need a larger garden. And when picked, a large container to display them. In a smaller garden, plant them at the back of the border, preferably in color groups for impact, but allow space for expansion and to let in enough light. The fans produce quite tall leaves and should be placed to catch maximum sun. In windy areas it might be necessary to stake the flower stems, but usually this is not needed. Flowering time is after the Intermediates.

Varieties recommended for vigor, health and mass flowering: 'Before the Storm' (Innerst 1989), incredibly black; 'Jazz Me Blue' (Schreiner 1993), ruffled rich marine blue; 'Alpine Journey' (Blyth 1984), white standards, golden falls; 'Elisa Renee' (Gaulter 1983), orchid pink with tangerine beard; 'Floral Art' (Grosvenor 1984), white standards, blue falls, red beard; 'Gypsy Romance' (Schreiner 1994), violet-mulberry with blue-purple beards; 'Honky Tonk Blues' (Schreiner 1998), ruffled blue-violet streaked and swirled with white.

Species

The amazing flowers we drool over today are hybrids, developed by years of sometimes planned, sometimes fortuitous hybridization. The different species from which they originated come mainly from Europe and the Mediterranean countries – collected and transported by early travelers – and seldom show any similarity to modern blooms. Yet it is their heritage

Tall Bearded *Iris pallida* look attractive planted with Rugosa rose seedlings.

that accounts for the differences in their growth habits, disease resistance, height and the characteristics of the flower. Zone information for iris species is not an effective predictor of growability. So many other factors come into play, such as high summer heat, extreme humidity, rainfall and local microclimates. Irises in North America can be very idiosyncratic, so look at the origin of the species as a clue to its preferred climate. A zone will be given when it is significantly different from the general range of zones 7-10 for these types of irises.

From southern Europe came **Iris pallida** of orrisroot fame, characterized by its paper-like flower spathes sheathing the buds and treasured for its glaucous blue-green foliage that stays handsome right through summer. Its flowers are soft mauve-blue, lilac or lavender. There is also a variegated form *I. pallida*

I. germanica is somewhat of a mystery. Many bearded iris species are listed under this name but it would appear to have become an umbrella term for a group of early hybrids that have naturalized in many countries and that flower in late winter or early spring, before the Tall Beardeds. Under this umbrella are some plants that have been given species ranking, including *I. florentina*, originally cultivated extensively in Italy for the production of orrisroot; *I. germanica* var 'Atropurpurea', introduced in the 19th century from Kathmandu, with red-purple flowers; and *I. squalens*, an early hybrid in shades of violet-gray, of interest to hybridizers because of its ruffled petal edges.

I. albicans is a native of Saudi Arabia and Yemen, growing in dry, rocky places up to 7200 ft (2200 m) above sea level. One of the ancestors of the Tall Beardeds, it still grows in colonies in several southern Mediterranean countries. It is an elegant flower, usually white and sweetly scented.

variegata, an excellent garden form with the advantage of variegated leaves to enjoy when the flowers are over for the season. *I. pallida* added height to the hybrid equation but offered very little in the way of branching genes.

I. mesopotamica from Armenia and Turkmenistan brought beautiful blues into the bearded irises as well as height and branching attributes, but it is frost tender in colder districts – a less desirable trait passed on to many hybrids that share its genes.

I. variegata comes from central Europe and the Balkans, and it is to this plant that we owe all the yellow tones in bearded irises. Those gardeners who like the old hybrid 'Gracchus' would see similarities in its pale yellow standards with white falls striped in red-purple. *I. flavescens*, also yellow and classed as a species, is probably a cross between *I. pallida* and *I. variegata*.

Similar to *I. albicans* is **I. kashmiriana** which comes, unsurprisingly, from Kashmir as well as India, Pakistan, Afghanistan and Nepal. Its flowers are also fragrant and have flaring falls. As a white tetraploid, it is of value in hybridizing programs.

I. albertii is a native of central Asia where it grows on rocky hillsides and grassy steppes. Its flowers are purplish blue, the beards white, tipped with yellow. It has widely branching stems to about 28 in (70 cm) in the wild, is early blooming, hardy and disease resistant. While it would probably appeal to few gardeners, its attributes are of great interest to hybridizers.

The small Dwarf Beardeds have been derived from many generations of crossbreeding among a large number of low-growing species, many of which are rare or unknown in cultivation. But **I. chamaeiris** (syn *I. lutescens*) is one that is easy to cultivate and

Tall Bearded 'Gallant Moment', brown-red, and 'Festive Skirt'.

rewarding to grow. It's an evergreen plant, forming dense mats, and comes with lovely dark red-purple flowers, or sometimes yellow, white or bicolored, arriving in early spring. It is hardy, likes full sun, good drainage and sets seed readily.

I. pumila is probably the best-known of the smaller bearded iris species but is not as accommodating as I. chamaeiris. It must have perfect drainage and the soil should be rich in lime. The unbranched flower stem (or more correctly, the perianth tube) grows to between ¹/₂-4 in (1.5-10 cm) – smaller even than I. chamaeiris – and is variable in form, size and color due to the vastness of its natural habitat across the former Soviet Union and central Europe. Colors range from shades of yellow and blue through lilac to purple, black and sometimes maroon or ruby red. As with the blooms of I. chamaeiris, the standards tend to be larger than the falls and curve gracefully over the style arms.

I. reichenbachii is another ancestor of the Dwarf Beardeds. A hardy plant, growing to about 12 in (30 cm), it is widespread in its natural habitat throughout Serbia, Bosnia, Bulgaria, Macedonia, Romania and Ukraine. Yellow is the predominant color, though it is also found in shades of lilac and purple, and it makes a showy display *en masse*.

I. suaveolens (syn I. mellita) is an attractive little plant, with flowers a shot-silk blend of bronze-brown and purple, with a tiny white beard stained blue at the tip. A native of hilly areas of Greece and other countries around the Mediterranean, it demands perfect drainage, loose rich soil and added lime.

Aril and Arilbred

These are bearded iris species from the very dry areas of Israel and Turkey and include Oncocyclus and Regelia irises as well as Arilbreds – hybrids derived from crosses made between Tall Beardeds and species in the above-mentioned groups. The name aril relates to the peculiarity of a small white aril or collar-like appendage attached to the seed. Arils are generally not easy to grow in temperate climates, preferring zones 7-8. In zone 9, for example, they tend to be susceptible to rust and to rhizome soft rot. Without a regular spray program, it is easy to lose them. However, low rainfall is the key factor in growing them successfully.

Quite different from other bearded irises, the Arils have fine, insignificant leaves that lack luster and vigor, in contrast to the lush green leaves of the standard bearded irises. But the flowers are spectacular, with interesting color patterns and shapes. The blooms of the Oncocyclus and Regelia are quite different from other bearded irises: the standards are rounded, almost closed together and quite large compared to the falls that recurve inwards under the flower.

The colors of the Arils can be very pure and clear, or the flowers can have amazing contrasting blotches on them. When crossed with bearded irises, some of these characteristics are retained and, in others, fascinating colors, streaks and patterns may emerge.

If your climate is very hot and dry in summer and cold in winter, and if you are determined, have lots of patience and are not easily depressed by failure, these could be worth a try. Place them with their faces to the sun and under the eaves of the house where they will get protection from any summer rain. And make sure they have perfect drainage. They grow to various heights and tend to be early flowering. Arilbreds are more likely than the species to do well in situations where Tall Beardeds grow well.

The following varieties grow fairly well in zone 9: Tall Bearded: 'Esther the Queen' (Hunt 1968), bluish green with maroon spot on falls; 'Tabriz' (Kidd 1983), lavender and tan with large purple signal. Intermediate: 'Bird Dancer' (Catton 1982), unusual green and gold blend; 'Haidie' (Catton 1979), lavender standards, falls flushed rose, brown hafts and purple beards; 'Wyuna Evening' (Catton 1987), lavender-pink-coffee, with brown hafts and bronze beards. Standard Dwarf Bearded: 'Fairy Goblin' (Foster 1967), smoky gray-green.

The best known (and easiest to grow) Oncocyclus species is **I. susiana**, sometimes called the mourning iris for its somber colors. Originally from Syria, it has been cultivated for 400 years but has never been found in the wild. How intriguing!

I. susiana

Flowers are large, towering over the foliage, and the colors unusual, with standards and falls of creamy gray background and heavy, close veining of dark purple-brown. The signal patch on the falls is rich velvety ruby-black and the beard a deep purple-bronze. Exciting or revolting, depending on your point of view!

Problem solving

Good leaf growth but no flowers.
- Check site: does plant get enough sun?
- Check climate: do other bearded irises flower well in the area?
- Check fertilizer: has the plant had too much nitrogen?
- Check depth of planting: does the rhizome itself get enough sun?
- Check variety: some flower more freely than others.

Poor all-around growth.
- Try transplanting to new soil.

Collapsing, yellowing plants.
- Check for rhizome rot.

CHAPTER 3

Evansia or Crested Irises

Those gardeners who have always thought of irises as tall, stately, richly hued plants may be surprised to discover the Evansia or Crested irises. For the group includes the smallest iris there is – a miniature whose flowers appear on stems mere inches above the ground. Others of the group form spreading evergreen clumps that look comfortable in a shrubbery and have orchid-like flowers produced on long springy stems. In spring they are starred with dozens of dainty flowers delicately frilled, their markings subtle. It is hard to imagine the relationship between these plants and the formal, highly bred bearded irises.

The distinguishing feature of all these irises (except one hard-to-find species) is the serrated, or toothed, crest on the haft of the fall where you find the beard on the bearded iris and the signal on Siberians, Louisianas or other beardless varieties. The crest may look rather like the cockscomb on a rooster (though not bright red), or it may be merely the suggestion of a raised furry patch, similar to those seen on Dutch or Spanish irises. It is usually a distinctive color or pattern.

Variable in size and height, they fall into two distinct groups: those that are dormant in winter and come mainly from North America, and the others, which are tender, sub-tropical, evergreen and native to Asia.

Why call them Evansias? As with so many plants, the name comes from the person who introduced them to the western world – never mind the plant's origins! All we know about him is his name and the fact that he worked for an English company in India. Was he an amateur botanist? Did he collect other plants and send them "home"? Whatever else he did, Thomas Evans was responsible for introducing *I. japonica* to England in 1794 and his name lives on.

Contrary to most irises, the Evansias (or orchid irises as they are sometimes known), will usually perform best in light shade. Hot sun or frost may burn the very broad, flat, strap-shaped leaves that many Evansias have and that add to their attraction.

Evergreen group

In mild temperate climates (zone 9), the evergreen Evansias are attractive, useful landscaping plants that look good even when they are not in flower. Several species make easy-care plants for gardeners who have other lives to live. They form clumps of distinctive foliage that add interest to the edges of woodland plantings where overhanging trees will protect them from frost and excessive hot sunshine.

In warmer areas (zones 9 and 10), they continue their growth nearly all year with very little dormancy in frost-free situations. Where winters are too cold for them to survive unprotected, they can be grown in containers, and then moved to shelter before the killer frosts arrive. They generally need no more care than the annual application of an all-purpose fertilizer and a protective sprinkling of snail bait around them in spring.

Opposite: Evansia 'Bourne Graceful'

I. japonica

Species

I. japonica is a native of China, where it grows as far west as Sichuan, flowering through April and May on grassy or rocky slopes in woodland and among rocks beside streams. It was given its misleading name after it became widely naturalized in Japan, originally arriving in that country as a gift from the Chinese Emperor to his Japanese counterpart.

I have seen it growing in a garden at the edge of rainforest among fern and native bush. It grabbed my attention with its wide strappy leaves and pale, mauve-blue flowers – like small orchids – decorated with darker violet dots and a tiny, white, orange-tipped crest. The mass of background bush enhanced its somewhat exotic appearance.

Dense clumps grow to 2 ft (60 cm) in height, with the flower spikes emerging above the leaves. The joy of this plant is its multi-branched spikes, each bearing many blooms over a period of five weeks, although flowering can be negatively affected by an exceptionally cold winter.

It will grow in full sun where there is no risk of frost, but expect the leaves to lose a lot of their gloss and become almost yellowish green; the flowers will be paler.

The plant has slender, creeping rhizomes and where it's not checked by severe frosts or drought, it will grow vigorously and increase quickly.

It delights in moist, rich, slightly acidic, loose, composty soil; it likes to be fed frequently – rotted manure is good – and needs to be well-drained. A shallow-rooting plant, divisions can be pulled away by hand from the main clump for replanting. This can be done successfully at any time of the year, though late spring is best.

If you live in a climate with no more than slight frosts and have a steep bank you want to keep free from intruders (or weeds) you might try growing *I. japonica*. In times gone by, it was encouraged in Japan around hilltop castles, as the slippery leaves slowed the advance of invaders and gave defenders time to muster their weapons!

There is a form bearing beautiful white flowers subtly marked in yellow and with deeply fringed ends on its style arms called *I. japonica* forma *pallescens*.

I. wattii is a native of Yunnan province in China. It is the tallest of the Evansias, with luxuriant foliage that develops as leaf fans growing from bamboo-like stems, reaching more than 5 ft (1.6 m) in height. Some growers recommend staking the flowering stems as they emerge at the first hint of spring, to keep the clump in shape and to prevent them from bending over with their own weight – understandable when you realize that the flowering spray can be 6 ft (2 m) tall. Each spray is branched and may produce up to 50 flowers during an eight- to 10-week period. With delicate, clear lavender flowers that are ruffled, frilled and almost 4 in (10 cm) across, a bush in bloom can be a spectacular sight.

This is not a plant to grow in windy, exposed areas for the flowers damage easily, as does the foliage, but it will sustain light frosts without harm.

Like *I. japonica*, it increases rapidly but remains tidier in shape. Divisions can be taken from the tough, side rhizomes at any time of the year. They lift out with roots intact, ready for planting. Propagation is also possible by taking cuttings from the stems. To do this, place pieces in water for a couple of weeks and new roots will appear from joints in the canes. The plant is not always long-lived, so it's a good idea to start new plants from time to time.

I. confusa is another of the Evansias with dainty orchid-like blooms. Originally confused with *I. wattii* when it was first introduced to England – hence the name – it is similar but does not grow as tall and the flowers, normally white with yellow and purple dots on the falls, are smaller. Another native of Yunnan, where it grows on steep slopes among rocks and scrub, it flowers in May and is hardy to zone 9 if given some shelter.

Though **I. tectorum** is another Evansia originating in China and the Himalayas, its flower differs from the preceding species, with a form less like an orchid and more reminiscent of the flat Japanese irises. It's a large bloom, about 4 in (10 cm) in diameter, soft blue-mauve with a prominent, white, toothed crest and standards that are only slightly elevated. Beautiful as the flower is, *I. tectorum* is best known for the traditional custom of planting it on roofs in Japan. Legend has it that Japanese women used to grind up the roots of the rhizome to make a face powder. When famine struck and they were forbidden to grow any plant in the fields that wasn't food, they planted the rhizomes in the roof thatch rather than go without their precious face powder.

Another explanation is that the iris roots were an excellent binding medium for the thatching at the apex of the roof. Certainly irises are used like this in France – a more picturesque solution than the terracotta tiles in Normandy, cemented together to hold modern thatch in place.

If you're lucky enough to have a dry stone wall in your garden, then plant *I. tectorum* along the top, though remember it will need some summer

I. wattii, handsome with camellias.

I. tectorum

moisture. It's grown this way in China and in late spring its mauve flowers sitting above fans of bright green foliage create an eye-catching fringe atop the gray stones.

In its native habitat *I. tectorum* enjoys dry cold winters and warm wet summers. A lower-growing species, it will stand more sun and much colder winters than the preceding Evansias, going almost dormant in cold climates. As you would expect with a plant that flourishes on roofs and walls, it likes perfect drainage and full sun. The roots are very shallow and, where happy, it increases fast, so divide it up every two or three years, give it a meal of sheep manure or enriched compost, and the plant will stay vigorous. Grown among stones it will probably need new soil added each year. It can be divided up as soon as spring flowering is over or, alternatively, as soon as the rains start in fall. Although generally frost hardy, young spring growth will be damaged by frost. There is also a white form of *I. tectorum* that comes true from seed.

I. milesii comes from the same regions as *I. tectorum* and grows up to 30 in (75 cm) tall. It favors similar soil conditions although it does not tolerate lime. It forms an attractive, vigorous clump of foliage, much more upright than *I. japonica* though the flowers, which appear in early summer, are more slender. Light pinkish purple in color and with more erect standards than in other Evansias, they appear on slender branched stems good for picking. This iris is dormant in winter, with all the foliage disappearing to leave the rhizomes lying on the surface of the soil, noticeable for their bright green color.

I. milesii

Cultivars and hybrids

There are numerous cultivars and hybrids of these dainty-flowered plants which vary in size and color – from white to blue-lavender. A few are listed below. They are all hardy to zone 9.

About 50 years ago, Jean Stevens, a well-respected New Zealand irisarian, crossed *I. wattii* with *I. tectorum* to produce the hybrid 'Queen's Grace'. The plant has large leaves and deep lavender flowers with a small pale yellow crest.

Two recent Evansia arrivals are *I.* 'Nova' and *I.* 'Chengdu'. The first of these two is a tall plant that sets seed reliably and has large white blooms marked with gold. It was found in a garden in the U.K., but has not yet been found in the wild.

I. 'Chengdu', however, came from China, via the U.S., and it appears from recent study that it might be a species in its own right. It has glossy, dark green leaves and deep lavender flowers with a prominent purple zone surrounding the white area adjacent to the deep yellow crest. Its growth habit is similar to *I. confusa* and is very similar to a variety named 'Martyn Rix'.

'Ledger's Variety' is common in Europe, first arriving in England in 1912 and sourced from the garden of the British Delegation in Tokyo. It has darker foliage; the flowers are similar to those of *I. japonica*, but they appear later in the season.

'Nada' has smaller, near-white flowers with a prominent bold yellow crest.

'Darjeeling' has more compact growth than *I. japonica*, black stems and spotted flowers with orange-tipped crests.

'Bourne Graceful', raised in 1966, is recognizable by its distinctive black stems that grow to 4 ft (120 cm) and bear beautiful frilly lilac flowers with a strong orange signal. It has no canes. Glossy dark green leaves have a purple smudge at the base of the fan.

I. cristata

Hardy group

This group comprises the babies of the Evansia family, though they have the same characteristics as their taller siblings. **I. cristata** is a miniature iris from the eastern United States where it grows in moist woods, banks and ledges with its rhizomes growing along the soil surface and arching off the ground. The rhizomes tend to swell towards the tip. It is very suitable for rock gardens but the clumps need to be lifted and divided occasionally, as they spread outwards, dying out in the center. It enjoys being cosseted with plenty of leaf mold, prefers partial shade in warm climates and likes a loose acidic soil. Provide it with good drainage and you should be rewarded with mats of strappy foliage produced as fans from small, branched rhizomes. Soft lilac-blue blooms, on flowering stems only 4 in (12 cm) high when the buds open, appear at the same height as the foliage though the leaves grow taller as the season progresses. The flowers are almost flat in form, about $1^1/_2$ -2 in (3-4 cm) across, bearing white crests tipped with gold.

Unusually, it is best to divide these just before they flower in early spring. If you must move the plants after flowering, try and remove the rhizomes from the edge of the main plant complete with a clump of soil, with as little root disturbance as possible.

Make sure the new plant does not dry out until it is well-established. Late summer or fall is a very risky time to divide *I. cristata*. The color of the flowers is variable; there are several forms of white as well as lavender-pink and a clear blue.

I. lacustris, the smallest of the Evansias, is found growing wild around the shores of the Great Lakes in Canada and in the central and northeastern states where it favors moist areas of sand or gravel, usually at the edge of cedar and fir woods, in partial shade. Take very good care of it in dry summers: it will not survive if it is allowed to dry out. It is even smaller than *I. cristata* and looks similar. The flowering stems grow only 2-3 in (5-7 cm) in height, and the flowers are almost sky-blue with a golden crest and a white patch on the falls. Though it demands similar conditions to *I. cristata*, it tends to be less robust. The tiny rhizomes are of even thickness, like fingers on a hand lying flat on the ground, and need protection from drying out. Mulching with plenty of leaf mold or compost works well and light overhead shade adds extra protection.

I. gracilipes is small and graceful, sometimes referred to as the daintiest of all irises. It comes from the mountains of Hokkaido, Honshu and Kyushu in Japan and is also found in China growing on wooded slopes. In very warm, dry areas, it needs protection from summer heat, for in full sun the foliage becomes almost yellow-green and the plant does not produce full-sized blooms. The flowers, in late spring, are lilac-blue with a mostly white crest, yellow at the apex. When it comes to division and transplanting, exercise the same care as with *I. cristata*, both for timing and making sure the divisions are not too small. Mulch any newly moved plants with leaf mold or enriched compost to protect the fine roots and keep the soil moist. As summer progresses the rhizomes tend to rise up out of the ground and if not protected by mulch they will dry out very quickly.

CHAPTER 4

Beardless Irises

A beardless iris conjures up a picture of a shaven, balder version of a bearded iris. But in fact this section includes species and cultivars of iris with widely differing habits, and flowers very different from the well-known bearded irises. Plants range in size from some of the smallest of the genus to the tallest Spuria irises that grow to over 6½ ft (2 m).

Nearly all the beardless irises have some distinguishing feature in place of the beard, or the distinctive crest of the Evansias. It may be a colored patch with complicated patterns, or a brightly colored signal that in some modern Louisianas can appear as a striking six-pointed star.

The beardless irises are divided into groups – or series, as irisarians refer to them – according to specific botanical details. Some of the groups are large, containing many species and hybrids. A few comprise only one species.

Ideal growing conditions are as variable as the plants themselves. This chapter discusses the different groups and their special attributes.

Spuria

If highly bred, frilled and fancy flowers are not to your taste then perhaps the Spuria irises, with their somewhat ascetic blooms, will be the type you choose to grow. It's not that they have escaped the notice of hybridizers: much breeding has been done with this tall species, especially in the U.S.A., and

A wild Spuria seedling.

some gorgeous color combinations have been achieved. But even the cultivars have retained the essence of the original flower shape with long, upright standards and long falls that flare out into a spoon shape. Both the standards and the falls may have become wider, lessening the rather spidery look of the species, but there's something clean and no-nonsense about the cultivars and species alike.

Often the colors are clear and intense, as in 'Sunny Day', a superb bright yellow; or 'Adobe Sunset', a rich gold with exquisite dark brown veining.

Opposite: Hybrid Japanese irises are elegant plants beside water.

Above left: Spuria 'Ping'. Above right: Hybrid spurias.

The group includes some of the tallest of the genus. Proud plants these, with the flowers massed above the foliage. They have a directness about them. You couldn't possibly stand round-shouldered in their presence. With strong, handsome, sword-like foliage (once used to make rope in Europe) and strong flower stems, they make tough, wind-resistant plants, excellent to grow as a vertical accent behind billowing perennials.

And then there are the small species, such as *I. sintenisii*, a dwarf Spuria that grows to no more than 12 in (30 cm). It looks attractive among rocks at the front of a border where there is little danger of losing it under taller plants.

The cylindrical seeds of this series are encased in a papery bag, inside a tough and pointed seed pod.

Culture

Spurias are native to Europe, North Africa and Asia. In the wild the species thrive in conditions as varied as salt marshes, open woodlands and sub-alpine slopes. Not the conditions that many gardeners can replicate, regardless of commitment! But in reality these irises are not difficult to cultivate. Although cold hardy (zones 6-9), they will do well in milder regions, their period of dormancy depending on temperature and availability of water. In warmer climates, new foliage will spring up almost immediately after the old has died down.

Plant them in heavy, slightly acidic soil, enriched with plenty of humus. Add rotted manure and ensure that drainage is good. Give them a dressing of balanced fertilizer in spring and a mulch of compost in fall. One grower, who has had great success with Spurias, treats them every fall to a light mulch of seaweed.

They like full sun and, although they need moisture for most of the year, there is a period after flowering when the tall varieties should be allowed to dry out until late summer. Paradoxically, the smaller species react badly to summer and fall droughts and it's important they are grown in soil that is well-drained but is not allowed to dry out. In warmer climates it is a good idea to give them partial shade.

their strong colors stand out among foliage plants. Their flowers have an unusual distinguishing feature, even after being cut: there are three nectar drops at the base of the falls and standards. Most tall modern Spurias are bred from *I. crocea* and *I. orientalis*.

Species

I. orientalis (formerly *I. ochroleuca*), is a salt marsh iris in its natural habitat. In cultivation it is one of the best-known Spurias. It grows to more than 3 ft (1 m), forming handsome clumps, with flower stems up to $4^1/_2$ ft (1.5 m) in damp conditions. Flowers are large and white, blotched on the falls with bright egg-yolk yellow.

I. crocea is another of the tall Spurias, a vigorous sunshiny plant from Kashmir, growing up to $4^1/_2$ ft (1.5 m). It flowers in early summer and the bright yellow blooms may reach 7 in (18 cm) in diameter. Falls are wavy or crinkly at the edges, standards are long and narrow. This is an easy one to grow in a sunny border in good rich soil.

I. spuria, which gives its name to the series, is difficult to describe because it is so variable. It ranges in height from 16-28 in (40-70 cm) and the colors of its flowers vary through shades of yellow, blue-mauve and white. They are slender in form,

Planting and division

Woody rhizomes and wiry roots characterize Spurias. Unlike other irises, the rhizomes grow from the same point each season. Most species have a wandering habit, with the new leaves appearing in winter or early spring from fat growth buds beyond the point where the previous season's growth emerged. Larger species are slow to increase.

Tough as these plants may be, they resent being moved and will often sulk for the first season after a shift, refusing to flower. If you must, divide the tall ones in fall, and the smaller species in early spring, and keep them well-watered.

Flower characteristics

The blooms of these irises are similar to Dutch and Spanish (or Xiphium) irises – those usually found in florists' shops – and, like the Xiphiums, they make excellent cut flowers. Frequently, the Spuria iris will open two or more flowers at the same time on long, usually unbranched stems. They flower in early summer, at the same time as the Tall Beardeds, and

I. pseudocyperus, a less common Spuria species.

daintily proportioned and bear fine veining on their falls. It is a native of Europe, from England through to Sweden, Hungary and the former Czechoslovakia, growing in wet meadows and salt marshes.

I. monnieri is considered to be an ancient hybrid of *I. orientalis* and *I. xanthospuria*. The flowers are slender and aristocratic with tall, very upright creamy standards while the falls are deeper yellow. Records show that it grew at Versailles in 1808 with the name of 'Iris de Rhodes' and was painted by Redouté. Apart from the color of its flowers, it is very similar to *I. orientalis*.

The following three species are all lower-growing.

I. graminea forms an attractive low clump with plenty of fine, grassy foliage in which the delightfully fruit-scented flowers nestle. It will grow in sun or semi-shade, enjoys rich moist soil and looks superb in a container, so long as it is not allowed to dry out. Several plants growing together make an excellent weed-suppressing group, though it is deciduous. The lilac-violet flowers, finely veined on the falls, appear in early summer. Though small, only $3^1/_2$ in (8 cm) across on stems about 8 in (20 cm) tall, they display the typical Spuria form.

I. sintenisii is another low-growing species, more dwarf and compact than *I. graminea* and very suitable for a rock garden. Unlike *I. graminea*, it is evergreen. Its flowers, in late spring or early summer, are blue-purple, on stems up to 12 in (30 cm) tall. Like some of its taller cousins this plant is reluctant to move and it's easy to damage the roots when dividing a clump.

The best time to transplant is in early spring or after rain in early fall. It needs plenty of moisture at its roots, preferring not to be baked dry in summer. In the Balkans and Turkey it grows wild in dry scrub and grass.

I. sintenisii

I. kerneriana is one of the most attractive of the small Spurias for the rock garden or front of the border. The height is about 12 in (30 cm). Flowers appear in late spring with slender blooms comprising creamy white standards and falls marked in deep yellow.

The dull green foliage is rather sparse in comparison to *I. graminea* and the flower stems overtop the foliage by several inches. It likes a sunny position in good, well-drained soil but should not be allowed to dry out when dormant in fall.

Pacific Coast or Californian

Delightful, dainty, beautifully colored, useful, promiscuous. Does this sound like somebody you know? If you are a dedicated iris grower then quite possibly you are familiar with the flowers that have been described in such terms by various growers. They are known as Californian irises and this of course gives the clue to their place of origin. You probably wouldn't mistake a flower from this group for a bearded iris, but some look very similar to modern Siberian blooms and there are others that could easily be mistaken for a Louisiana. They hybridize very freely among themselves and, as with

Pacific Coast seedling.

The rich color of a Pacific Coast seedling contrasts with euphorbia and forget-me-nots.

many other groups of iris, they have received a lot of attention from hybridizers, particularly Joe Ghio in the U.S., who has concentrated on producing blooms that are of beautiful rounded form with ruffled petals. The many and often unaccountable hybrids are now commonly called Pacific Coast irises.

It is possible to find these plants growing wild along the Pacific Coast from southern California to Oregon on open grassy slopes and partially shaded hillsides, or on the ground beneath trees in a mixed forest.

One species, *I. purdyi*, is not much taller than a toddler's knee and grows in redwood forests in northwest California. The blooms are dainty and creamy white, finely overlaid on the falls with red-brown veining – it is difficult to imagine a more complete contrast between it and the dark conifers towering overhead.

Plant characteristics

All the species in the group have tough slim rhizomes and grassy leaves. These are small irises, generally evergreen, which flower in early spring, right at the time when the Dwarf Beardeds are in full flower.

Even in the wild there is a huge range of colors, increased now with systematic hybridizing, in almost every imaginable shade from white through lilac, peach, purple, pink, blue, yellow, brown, orange and a wine-red. Often the falls display intricate patterns and designs.

When you need a rest from the vivid colors of spring, there are golden-tan combinations available that hold an eternal appeal for many gardeners.

These are among the lower-growing varieties of iris, with most of the hybrids growing from 10-16 in (25-40 cm) in height. They are useful plants to follow spring bulbs and to add splashes of color to a rockery.

Culture

Free-flowering and free-seeding, Pacific Coast irises, while hardy to zone 7, do not like high summer heat, wet feet or extreme humidity. Make sure the soil is well-drained with lots of grit and leaf mold incorporated into it. They like a neutral to slightly acidic growing medium – where rhododendrons and azaleas thrive, so too will Pacific Coast irises – and they will even tolerate soil that is fairly rich in calcium so long as no lime is added. In soils that tend to be acidic, an occasional light dressing of dolomite will help maintain the balance. Top-dress these irises from time to time with compost.

Attractive plants to grow under deciduous trees, they like partial shade with afternoon sun. They are happiest in climates where there are winters with plenty of rain continuing into spring, followed by hot dry summers.

Planting and division

Everyone who grows these delightful flowers seems to fall in love with them, but they present one common difficulty: they are very temperamental about being moved. "Sudden Death Syndrome" is one grower's description. In theory, they are ready to be moved when their thick white roots are visible, in early spring or in the fall. It may be necessary to scratch around in the earth a little to check out the root growth.

In older clumps the roots form a fine fibrous mat that is hard to separate, and without fresh young roots to get them going in a new position these old clumps often find it difficult to re-establish themselves once divided. Not so different from people really. Their best chance of transplanting

satisfactorily is when plentiful rain is expected.

Sometimes, however, it is possible to break all the rules and still find success. One experienced New Zealand grower mourns her lack of luck with moving Pacific Coast irises, yet has watched her daughter take a spade, slice cavalierly under a clump and successfully transplant half of it to another garden!

If you are one of the unlucky ones, leave your mature clumps undisturbed and start new plants from seed. It sets easily and germinates freely. Sown in fall, it's not difficult to raise. Left to their own devices, pods will scatter seed around your carefully selected parent plants and you'll find a variety of colors and sizes when these seedlings mature.

Seedlings come up with frail grass-like foliage but should not be planted out into permanent positions until little rhizomes have formed, which will take several months.

Species

There are about 12 species in this group, with four having made important contributions to the range of hybrids.

I. douglasiana and *I. innominata* are among the best-known of the Pacific Coast irises. With beautiful flowers borne on branched stems, *I. douglasiana* makes a good garden plant. Its native habitat is a narrow coastal strip from southern California to Oregon, where it flowers between March and May.

The flower color varies from pale cream to bluish or deep red-purple on stems growing to 24 in (60 cm). This is the tallest of the Pacific Coast irises, and grows easily in moist, peaty or sandy soil, but does not like to be fed with animal manure. It's a hardy plant, sun-tolerant and vigorous and it bears lots of flowers.

I. douglasiana

I. innominata starts to bloom in early spring and continues over six weeks, with established clumps providing a burst of color. Within the species there is a wide range of colors, from pale yellow to apricot, shades of brown and bronze, to pale lavender and deep purple. Both falls and standards are fairly wide, forming a flattish flower. The foliage is evergreen, although in its first winter the plant may lose most of its leaves. Late-season branching is a feature of some seedlings and this factor, combined with a large number of flower spikes, is a reason for their prolific flowering habit. Sun-tolerant and frost-tolerant, *I. innominata* likes rich, well-drained acidic soil, moisture in springtime, and drier conditions in summer. Grow a variety of clumps in the garden and the blooming season can extend for more than two months.

I. tenax, a native of Oregon and Washington, is easily grown. It is hardy and sun-tolerant with foliage that dies down in winter. The flowering spikes are unbranched, each one producing a slender-petaled, delicate flower with precise penciled markings and colors ranging through yellow, mauve, blue-lavender and purple. True-bred species are hard to find as it hybridizes in a promiscuous fashion.

I. bracteata is also dormant in winter with fresh foliage appearing in spring. Flowers are large and yellow on spikes up to 14 in (35 cm) tall. It comes from southern Oregon and is not very vigorous.

I. chrysophylla is another native of Oregon. An evergreen, its flowering spikes are compact, bearing two usually creamy white flowers veined in yellow, though shades of lavender and purple also occur.

Cal-Sibs

In recent years crosses have been made between Californian (Pacific Coast) and Sino-Siberian irises, facilitated by their similar chromosome count. Their cultivation requirements are similar to those of their parents but in warmer climates, where Siberians do not prosper because of lack of winter chill, and in climates where Californians are not hardy, these hybrids help to fill a gap.

Laevigata and other water-loving irises

It is difficult to imagine a more arresting garden sight than a group of tall elegant irises, in bloom, beside water. It may be the species *I. pseudacorus* with slender foliage and small, classic-shaped yellow flowers; it might be a clump of evocative Japanese irises with big flaring flowers, or it may be some brightly colored Louisianas. But the image it leaves in the mind is likely to last for a long time.

In fact there are various irises that thrive in a moist environment. From a cultural point of view it is important to distinguish between those that are true water irises and those that love water but also require a degree of drainage. All will grow in an ordinary garden situation provided they are supplied with plentiful water at the right season.

Species

I. laevigata, with its smooth strap-like leaves, is a true water iris and can be planted in soil right in

Below: *I. laevigata* 'Shirasagi'

I. laevigata 'Colchesterensis'

water where it may grow to a height of up to 6½ ft (2 m) and bear large flowers. Both height and flowering potential are dependent on rich soil and damp conditions. It is a delightful plant for those blessed with a private lake. But don't despair if this is not you. These days it is easy to include a water feature in the tiniest landscape and if you can't stand waterlilies hiding the water you've carefully captured, choose this beauty to flower above it and enjoy its reflections.

Plant the iris in a bucket or large planter bag, adding plenty of well-rotted animal manure or a balanced fertilizer. Anchor the container in the lake, pond or water-barrel, ensuring it is covered by no more than 2 in (5 cm) of water.

In the species, flowers are blue-violet with broad pendent falls marked by a central ridge of light yellow. There is also a white form. Cultivars flower in a range of colors from white to deep blue-purple. *I. laevigata* dislikes lime, preferring an acidic soil and as a gross feeder will need re-potting frequently. Avoid fertilizer that is too rich in nitrogen. One commercial grower, wishing to encourage his *I. laevigata* 'Colchesterensis' after its prodigious flowering efforts one season, decided to feed his plants liberally the following year with a slow-release all-purpose fertilizer, high in nitrogen. The results were disastrous!

In the garden, plant the rhizomes about 1 in (3 cm) below the surface of the soil, ensuring that the soil at the roots is always wet. Remember to give it an annual top-up in winter with well-rotted manure.

As a deciduous plant its regrowth starts about the middle of spring. Transplant it in early fall in a garden situation; in a bog situation it prefers being transplanted after flowering, in late spring or early summer.

I. laevigata 'Albopurpurea Colchesterensis' is a cultivar for those who look for drama. Deep, almost navy blue, it is starred in the center with bold white markings.

I. pseudacorus, or yellow flag, is a native of Britain and flowers in early summer. It blooms prolifically with plenty of water, boasting several branches on every plant and several flowers in each socket on every branch. With such a vigorous flowering habit it sets seed easily and germinates readily. In some climates it will quickly colonize large areas of swamp or bog and make a determined effort to reclaim a shallow lake in record time. Surprisingly, it is also tolerant of dry conditions, though it definitely prefers poorly drained, damp areas. This is one to grow in a tub where it can be kept under control. Like fire, it is a good servant but a poor master.

There are several cultivars of the species with flowers ranging from pale sulfur yellow (*I. pseudacorus bastardii*), through rich clear yellow without the dark markings typical of the species (*I. pseudacorus superba* 'Golden Queen'), to pale, almost white (*I. pseudacorus* 'Ivory').

'Holden Clough', declared by Roger Phillips and Martyn Rix in their book *Perennials* to be a chance hybrid between *I. chrysographes* and *I. pseudacorus*, has flowers of dull gold, with fine markings in brown-purple. Unlikely ever to win a beauty contest, its understated elegance is nevertheless fascinating. Definitely a flower for those who scorn the ordinary.

I. versicolor 'Kermesina'

I. virginica

I. pseudacorus 'Variegata' is valuable for its striking foliage of green and gold arranged in neat vertical stripes. In spring, beside water in which yellow bog primulas are in flower, the leaves alone are stunning.

I. versicolor is another true water iris, native to the northeast and midwest of the U.S.A. Where conditions are good for *I. pseudacorus*, they will also suit *I. versicolor*. It is among the smaller irises, with broad, heavily ribbed foliage and branched spikes each carrying several blooms.

The flowers are dainty, usually in shades of purple, mauve, blue-purple or lavender with a white splash on the falls and delicate veining in the main color. The falls tend to be narrower and more widely spaced than in many other iris blooms.

Old clumps can be divided in fall or early spring, although where it is grown in water, division after flowering is more successful. It grows easily from seed. *I. versicolor* 'Kermesina', with lovely rose-purple flowers, is an especially handsome garden plant.

I. virginica, also known as blue flag, is found mainly in the central to southwest U.S. It is slightly taller than *I. versicolor* and is more demanding. It prefers wet acidic soil with plenty of humus, dislikes cold conditions and flowers in early summer. Although variable in height, its spikes, usually unbranched, can reach 36 in (90 cm). Flowers are blue-violet through blue-purple, though seedlings come in a wider range of colors including white, shades of pink and sometimes maroon.

Cultivar 'Gerald Darby' (*I. versicolor* x *I. virginica*) attracts attention in spring when its leaves are young and stained at the base of its foliage with a wonderful purple. Flowers are blue-violet, delicately veined with a blush of yellow on the falls; hafts of the falls are long, giving the flower a delicate, though some may say a rather spidery, appearance.

Japanese

Despite the fascination, even awe, that irises have inspired in gardeners over the centuries, probably nowhere else have they achieved the cult status that is reserved for them in Japan. Although originally a simple water-loving species, the Japanese iris has been highly bred over the last 500 years to produce flowers of breathtaking beauty and, in the case of Higo iris, with one primary purpose in mind – that of indoor display.

In a highly ritualized ceremony with strict rules,

along the lines of the tea ceremony and the specialized schools of flower arranging, a potted plant would be brought inside when the bloom was ready to open. There, to emphasize the beauty of the usually pure white or rich single color, it was displayed in front of a gold screen, to be watched, over a period of three days of quiet meditation, as the flower gradually opened to its ultimate beauty.

The impressions left by this experience were said to be so profound that the watcher would be influenced for life. Not surprisingly, with today's increased pace of life, this practice is now much less common than in former times.

Long ago, however, the species *I. ensata* grew wild all over Japan, fulfilling a much more basic purpose. In the days before calendars, farmers would rely on seasonal changes to guide them in the growing of their rice crops. When the cherry trees blossomed it was time to start cultivating their fields. When the iris bloomed, the rainy season had arrived and it was time to transplant their rice plants from seedbed to paddy.

Inspired by the elegance of these simple flowers, Japanese hybridizers began experimenting with natural selections and cross-pollination as early as the 17th century. By the end of the 19th century superior new cultivars were being exported to the United States.

Also, in the latter part of that century, public gardens flourished around Tokyo where irises were

Japanese 'Ocean Mist'

grown in the paddy fields. City dwellers, seeking a brief respite from their crowded lives, would pay to view them. Gradually, three different strains of Japanese iris, each with its own characteristics, became recognized. Those developed in the paddy fields over a long period of time were named Edo, the ancient name for Tokyo. They produced flowers of great variation in size, color and form.

The Ise strain, named for the district of their origin, about 50 miles southeast of Kyoto, was developed primarily for growing in containers. Their

Diagram 3: Recognized Japanese iris flower forms

Single

Double

Multi-petaled or peony form

Japanese 'Pastel Princess'

blooms tend to be single in form with the falls in a pendent or hanging position.

Higo is an old province in Kyushu, and the irises developed there derived from the Edo varieties. They were also developed for containers, grown outside but brought indoors when they were ready to flower. Perfection of bloom was all-important, and because there was little interest in their garden performance, the development of plants with branching stems that produced a succession of flowers was unimportant.

Once the Higo strain became generally available and exported to the West, there was an increased interest in breeding these beautiful flowers for outdoors, though many cultivars were lost during World War II. Successive breeders, in both Japan and the U.S., have made crosses between the three strains and now, as the distinctions are fading, it is convenient to call them all by the term Japanese iris.

Culture

They are a hardy breed. Currier McEwen in his book *The Japanese Iris* says: 'Japanese irises are adaptable to a wide range of climatic conditions so long as their particular needs are met. They are extremely hardy to cold.' He adds that in Siberia they survive winter temperatures as low as −50°F (−45°C) though the effect of such bitter cold is tempered by an insulating blanket of snow. However, rapid cycles of freezing and thawing can damage modern cultivars. Hardiness ranges from zones 4-10.

Like most of us they don't enjoy wind and nothing is more disheartening than seeing long-awaited delicate blooms suddenly devastated by gales. So provide them with shelter. They thrive in full sun but appreciate partial shade when temperatures are very high.

Ample water from spring until late summer is the most important cultural requirement of Japanese iris – remember the species *I. ensata* growing in the paddy fields flooded in spring. A buried perforated irrigation hose laid in a garden bed where Japanese irises are planted is one way to ensure they are kept damp during the growing season.

Japanese 'Enchanted Lake'

Plenty of good food comes a close second to ample moisture. They are gross feeders and like a rich diet. Provide them with well-composted cow manure and ensure that the soil they grow in contains plenty of organic material – compost, spent straw, leaf litter – which will help to retain moisture while encouraging the rhizomes to grow deep strong roots.

These irises detest lime. Where soils are too alkaline, this can be remedied with a light top-dressing of sulfur. Mulch with peat, pine forest litter and leaf mold to help boost the acidity of the soil as well as provide a moisture-retentive covering.

Feed the plants in spring when the new leaves are about 3 in (8 cm) tall, and again after blooming.

Planting and division

Like any herbaceous perennial, Japanese irises die down and rest in winter and they will not tolerate waterlogged or boggy conditions while they are dormant.

Early fall is the best time for division and transplanting as this allows time for the rhizomes to form new roots that anchor the plant well in the soil before winter. However, with care, Japanese irises can be planted or transplanted at any time. In Japan they are frequently transplanted straight after flowering but in areas where summer drought is a problem, this is not a good idea.

Similarly, in areas that experience severe winter frosts, the more traditional fall planting may not allow the rhizome enough time to establish roots before frosts cause dislodging of the plants. Wait until spring.

Before transplanting during the growing cycle, thoroughly water the plant. Unearth the clump and cut out any damaged rhizomes, then trim back the foliage to about half its length to compensate for the loss of some roots.

Once the plant is prepared, dig a hole, spread well-rotted manure in the bottom and plant the iris on a mound of soil in the hole. Spread the roots well and ensure that the crown is $1^{1}/_{2}$-3 in (4-8 cm) below the surface – unlike bearded irises where the rhizome should not be totally buried.

After replanting, keep it very wet until the plant is well-established. All the water-loving irises are lime-haters, so avoid chicken manure and mushroom compost as these both contain lime.

Japanese irises enjoy the water's edge where their roots are naturally in moist soil, but beware of the risk of waterlogging during winter. Planted like this

Japanese 'Syokko'

they can remain undisturbed for years. However, grown in containers in ponds, they must be removed in the fall and replaced in late winter or early spring, once the new shoots have appeared.

Grown in garden situations, Japanese irises perform best when they are lifted every 3-4 years, trimmed of dead and unhealthy rhizomes and roots, and replanted in a bed that has had lots of composted manure added to it.

Flower characteristics

Talk about Japanese irises today and most people visualize a tall flamboyant plant beside water, with blooms flaring like an ice skater's skirt, probably white or delicately shaded in tones of mauve and purple. A brazen floozy to some maybe, but certainly a different lady from the demure flower that originally inspired Japanese farmers to plant out their rice seedlings.

The flower of the species is of a single form, with three upright small standards and longer pendent falls – the classic form still much admired by the Japanese and many purists. But frequently hybrids come in double form, with large standards, similar in size and appearance to falls that are broad and arranged horizontally, forming a large flat flower seemingly of six petals, almost circular in shape and sometimes frilled around the circumference.

Deviating even further from the species are some modern hybrids of multi-petaled or peony form where there are more than six 'petals' and the effect is of a much fuller flower.

In 1960 the first Japanese tetraploid cultivar (a plant engineered to have a double chromosome count) was bred by Currier McEwen in the United States, from *I. ensata*. Tetraploid cultivars have been available since 1979, and as more breeders succeed with this technique, the selection of flowers with exotic characteristics has increased.

The color range of white, blue, mauve, purple and pink may at first sound limited. But these irises come also with a huge variety of patterns. Most are

Japanese 'Cascade Spring Dress'

Japanese 'Pink Frost'. Below: Japanese 'Electric Rays'

The striped foliage of *Iris ensata* makes an attractive planting beside a small pool.

marked with a distinctive yellow signal on the falls, in place of the beard on bearded irises. In addition they may be veined with very fine, dark lines; they may be sanded – covered with small darker dots and very short broken lines; they may be brushed with minute dots, or edged around the falls and petals, or splashed with bold markings in white.

The immense range of shades available in each separate color makes it easy to achieve magical effects with mass plantings.

Blooming

Japanese irises extend the flowering season of the genus well into summer in some areas. When the glory of the Tall Beardeds is just a memory for another year, when the first flowering of the Siberians is almost over, it is then that the Japanese display their beauty. By choosing a selection of early-blooming to late-blooming varieties, gardeners can enjoy these irises for a season of about six weeks.

Some cultivars will produce a second blooming that occurs about three weeks after the flowers of the first flush have faded. Seed pods and flowers

therefore appear simultaneously on one plant. The ability to produce a second round of flowers, or remontancy, is dependent on the growing conditions but is a genetic feature of the plant. It will not happen merely because the plant has been pampered.

Species

I. ensata (syn *I. kaempferi*) (zone 6). This is the original parent from which the Japanese bred their large-flowered forms and is distinguished by its heavily ribbed thick foliage. Not a true water or bog plant, it prefers rich, well-drained soil but requires copious water in spring and early summer. Garden forms must have good drainage and rich, loose soil.

It grows to a height of about 42 in (1.3 m) and the flower stem extends well beyond the foliage. The flower varies from dark red-purple through to white and shades of blue, with a narrow gold median stripe on the fall.

Siberian

If you're looking for a perennial with graceful form, attractive supple foliage that stays green all summer and flowers of a breath-catching loveliness, then look no further than the Siberian irises. These are plants that form fountain-like clumps after several years with flowers that look like exotic butterflies fluttering above the foliage. And, as if their beauty were not sufficiently tempting, most are easy to raise and even easier to maintain. They're practical plants for the non-fanatic gardener – they will still flower if they're not fed, they will continue to perform if they're not divided and they're not too fussy about soil. Hardy through zones 3-10.

Not a true water iris they nevertheless enjoy damp conditions during their growing season and can stand flooding for short periods.

Like other water-loving irises Siberian irises look particularly elegant grown beside streams or ponds, but they can be naturalized in a field where they will grow happily year after year. I have seen a planting of 'Caesar's Brother' in full bloom, designed to form a long, wide, sinuous swath sweeping into the distance beneath silver birches. In the evening the western light emphasized the lustrous rich purple of the flowers – an unforgettable sight.

'Caesar's Brother' was bred before 1930 and

bigger brighter flowers have superseded it in popularity, but its beauty remains incontestable.

There are two distinct groups of Siberian irises. The first group consists of two species, each with 28 chromosomes, called the Sibirica series. They are **I. sibirica**, common throughout central Europe and Asia, where it naturalizes in damp meadows and reed swamps, and **I. sanguinea**, which is actually native to Siberia.

Records show that *I. sibirica* was growing in the Chelsea Physic Garden by 1600 while *I. sanguinea* was cultivated a little later in Japan, and became known in Europe by the second half of the 18th century.

The second group, consisting of eight species each naturally containing 40 chromosomes, is called the Chrysographes series or Sino-Siberians. A characteristic of the flowers of this group is the presence of two small flanges that curl up near the bases of the falls. Another typical feature is the hollow stem in most of the species, which makes

Left: Siberian 'Over to Gloryland'
Below: Siberian 'Summer Skies'

Above: White Siberian 'Crystal Charm'.
Right: Siberian 'Sky Mirror', a recent hybrid.

absolutely no difference to their appearance but is useful for identification.

Culture

I. sibirica and *I. sanguinea* comprise the hardier group. They require less moisture and are more tolerant of alkaline soils than the Chrysographes series. In general, all the Siberians need a rich, moist, acidic soil to thrive. Although they like water they will drown if continually submerged; reasonably good drainage is necessary.

When preparing a new bed, add plenty of composted manure, peat and a light dressing of sulfur if the soil pH is above 6.5. Where soils are sandy or clay, add compost and other organic material to increase the humus content and help retain moisture.

Not surprisingly when you think of their origins, Siberian irises are spectacular in cold climates. Both *I. sibirica* and *I. sanguinea* withstand extreme cold.

In temperate climates with plentiful rain they also do well, although the flower size and the height of the flower spike may be reduced. 'Caesar's Brother', and the much newer tetraploid hybrid 'Emma Ripeka', bred by New Zealander Frances Love in 1995 and a Dykes Medal winner, are both good cultivars for milder climates.

Hot dry conditions are not to their liking. Gardeners who relish a challenge and want to grow Siberians in such a climate need to provide partial shade, a good mulch and extra water.

In their natural climate zones, the Siberians like full sun. They will grow in shade but will usually refuse to flower. Nor do they like being blasted by wind. Once they are well-established, clumps can withstand periods of drought in late summer or fall.

Yellowing of the leaves may mean insufficient nitrogen or a lack of iron. This can be aggravated by poor soil acidity. Treat iron deficiency with iron chelate.

These are deciduous plants and once the foliage turns brown in the fall it is a good idea to cut it off and dispose of it by burning – if your area allows.

Planting and division

When it comes to planting Siberian irises, make allowances for your climate. Early fall is the traditional time to plant, especially where you can expect winter rain. However, excessive cold will inhibit root growth and heavy frosts may cause the rhizomes to be dislodged if the root structure is not well enough developed to anchor them firmly in the earth before the freeze sets in.

Spring is the time when the new rhizomes and roots actively grow, and given the right conditions new plants will develop quickly. But if you live in an area where spring is followed by long, hot, dry summers, make sure you are willing to water long and often if you want to make successful divisions at this time of the year.

In reality Siberian irises can be planted, or divided and replanted, at any time. Many buyers

Siberian 'Jewelled Crown'

want to see the flowers before they commit their dollars and it is often more satisfying to get the instant result of buying a plant in flower. If this is you, just remember to water! When you remove your new plant to the garden from its growing bag or pot, make sure the roots are never allowed to dry out until the plant is well established.

Dividing established clumps can be a mission. Theoretically, the idea is to approach the excavated clump with two long-handled garden forks and plenty of energy. Place the forks back to back, jab them into the center of the clump, then wrench – and hope it's the rhizomes that give way, not your muscles.

When you finally succeed, get rid of the spent rhizomes, old roots and the central part of the clump. It's the vigorous young outer portions you want to replant. Most growers find that small divisions take longer to reach their full flowering potential. So make sure that wrench is powerful!

The planting hole should be at least 10 in (25 cm) deep and enriched with composted manure mixed into the soil. As with Japanese irises, sit the new plant on a mound, spread out the roots and fill the hole, making sure the crown is 1-2 in (2-4 cm) below the surface of the soil once the planting is completed. Another feed after flowering will make the plant feel cherished and willing to perform again the following year. Mulching will help to retain precious moisture.

Seed pods ripen in mid-summer. Germination is quick and while rhizome division ensures offspring with the same characteristics as the parent plant, you may discover interesting variations in any seedlings that appear in the garden.

Flower characteristics

Much serious hybridizing has been done using the species in both groups, resulting in flowers of a very wide color range: white, cream, shades of yellow and even orange; every imaginable shade between blue and purple, some almost red and some true bitones and bicolors.

Until the late 1950s, Siberian iris cultivars were all characterized by pendent falls, typical of the species. But flowers with flaring, horizontal and rounded falls were created when Fred Cassebeer produced 'White Swirl' in 1957, selected from the thousands of seedlings he had raised. A refined bloom, satiny white with a subtle lemon marking on the haft of the falls, it has an element of fantasy that's been bred into succeeding generations of Siberian irises.

As with Japanese irises, tetraploids have been bred over the last 30 years and the larger, fuller flowers thus produced have strayed far from the species shape of narrow pendent falls and upright standards. The tetraploid cultivars also tend to be a stiffer plant, so the image of fluttering butterflies is less applicable to these flowers.

Increased hybridizing has led to a wide diversity of plant habit. Now there are true miniatures available, with flowers of 2¹/₂ in (7 cm) or less on spikes that range from 6-18 in (15-45 cm). At the other end of the scale there are plants with flower

Above left: Seedling Siberian iris.
Above right: 'Foretell' is an interesting older hybrid Siberian.

spikes over 48 in (120 cm) tall and flowers, ruffled and rounded, the size of saucers.

Blooming

To enjoy a real feast of iris blooms in the garden grow both Tall Beardeds and Siberians, as their flowering seasons overlap at the end of spring.

The average Siberian cultivar will produce two or three branches, each with several flowers blooming in succession. Each flower will look good for between two to four days, depending on the weather.

As with other types of iris, a careful choice of cultivars and/or species will ensure a flowering season spreading over several weeks. Some cultivars have been bred to repeat bloom within a few weeks after the first flush, an ability that is enhanced by ample water and fertilizing both before and after the first blooming period.

Siberian irises will not always flower in the first season after planting or replanting. So be patient.

Like wine and women, they improve with each passing year!

Species

I. sibirica grows naturally across Europe from western France and Switzerland, through Russia, the former Yugoslavia, Bulgaria, northern Turkey and the Caucasus. Dormant in winter, the grassy, graceful foliage appears in spring; typically the flower is blue-violet, attractively highlighted at the base (haft) of the falls with a white mark, veined in the main color. The flower stems are taller than the leaves – often reaching over 32 in (80 cm) – ensuring visibility. This is the archetypal "butterfly" Siberian, its flowers are delicate, slender in profile, with pendent falls and stiff upright standards.

I. sanguinea, native to Siberia, China, Korea and Japan, is similar to *I. sibirica*, but the flower spike is shorter and carries no branches. The flowers, though larger than those of *I. sibirica*, do not appear above the foliage and are darker in color – a deeper red-purple with heavier veining on the haft of the fall.

I. chrysographes is quite simply stunning. Slender, refined, understated, it is a native of China, Burma and Tibet and was collected by Ernest Wilson in Sichuan in 1908. The flowers are a rich purple with fine gold markings resembling an ancient script, hence its name. See it, and a Buddhist monk springs to mind, patiently scribing characters onto velvety petals for some sacred purpose. The flowers, delightfully fragrant, appear in late spring or early summer. There is a form, var *rubella*, with flowers of a reddish wine, and a black form – to die in debt for.

I. clarkei, another species from the roof of the world – Nepal, Tibet, India and Burma – was brought to the West after being collected in 1875 near Darjeeling, by Charles Baron Clarke. Untypically, it has solid stems. Flowers, with pendent falls and almost horizontal standards, range in color from violet through blue, appearing on up to three branches in early summer. Its foliage is wide and glossy.

In some areas in the eastern Himalayas it is said to be so plentiful and widespread that it is cut and dried for fodder for horses and yaks.

I. bulleyana photographed in the wild in China.

I. delavayi, a native of China, was brought to the West in the 1890s by a French missionary, L'Abbé de la Vaye, who discovered it in 1884, growing in swamps in Sichuan. It is one of the tallest species in the group, growing to 5 ft (150 cm), and has the widest foliage. The spike is well branched, with six or seven dark violet blooms, each bearing white veins and a signal patch. The falls are pendent and the standards are almost horizontal.

A swamp-dweller, it makes an ideal bog garden plant, flowering in early to mid-summer. It is easy to raise from seed but needs to be hand-pollinated as it has promiscuous habits.

I. forrestii, another introduction from China, collected by George Forrest in Yunnan province in 1908, and *I. wilsonii*, collected in western China in 1907 by Ernest Wilson, are both plants of alpine pastures and rocky hillsides, growing at altitudes up to 13,000 ft (4300 m). They have yellow, scented flowers, two to a stem, that appear in mid-summer.

I. wilsonii grows to about 30 in (75 cm), has gray-green leaves and the rather large, pale yellow flower is decorated with violet veining on the falls. It is more robust than *I. forrestii*, flowers later in the summer and its leaves are as tall as the flower stems.

I. forrestii is much shorter, attaining 14-16 in (35-40 cm) in height. The leaves are shiny on one side, dull on the other and much shorter than the flower stems.

Its color is a clearer yellow than *I. wilsonii*, with narrower falls faintly veined. Initially the standards are erect but they soon curl outwards. Less vigorous than the other Sino-Siberians, it is important to water during late summer to prevent it drying out.

The last four species in this group are less significant in the contribution they have made towards garden cultivars.

I. bulleyana comes from China and in the past there have been doubts about its heritage, with some thought that it may be a hybrid of *I. chrysographes* and *I. forrestii*. However, with increasing numbers of plant seekers exploring in China, new finds indicate that it is a species in its own right but with variable forms.

It is compact, reaching about 16 in (40 cm) in height and, in the best-known form, the standards and the tips of the slightly rounded falls are dark indigo blue, while the center is white with deep blue spots and veins.

I. dykesii is perhaps another hybrid and is like a vigorous form of *I. chrysographes*, with bright, deep violet flowers that have white and yellow fall markings. It is not known in the wild and is rare in cultivation.

I. typhifolia, a sibling of *I. chrysographes*, has recently become available for cultivation. It's a slender, elegant plant with very tall, twisty, thin foliage and its dark blue flowers with long pendent falls encourage growers to keep persevering even in the face of its reluctance to flower every season.

I. phragmitetorum was once collected in the Yunnan province of China but is unknown in cultivation.

Louisiana 'Red Gamecock'. The tiny dark square cells visible in the foliage are a mark of a true water iris.

Louisiana or Hexagona irises

In Europe, the stately form of iris flowers has been recorded for hundreds of years; in Egypt and the Mediterranean this can be extended to thousands. Ancient works of art preserve stylized forms of *I. pseudacorus*, the flag iris, and *I. germanica*, an ancestor of our modern bearded irises. Use of these plants for medicinal purposes is well-documented. But in the southern United States there exists a group of irises that aroused little botanical interest until about one hundred years ago, though no doubt the plants were admired for centuries previous by Indians.

Generally known as Louisiana irises, they bloom in spring, usually April–May in the northern hemisphere and October–November in the southern hemisphere.

The many varied cultivars that exist today have been bred from the five species and their natural hybrids, most of which come from the Mississippi Basin, though one, *I. hexagona*, is native to the swamps of Florida, Alabama and Georgia. Named for the six prominent ribs on its seed cage, it gives its name to the group and was first described in 1788.

Louisiana 'Byron Bay'

Descriptions of the species *I. fulva* and *I. brevicaulis* followed some years later. But the remaining two species in this group were not described until last century: *I. giganticaerulea* in 1929 and *I. nelsonii* in 1966, after being "discovered" during the late 1930s.

In the early 1900s, these irises grew in great profusion in the swamps and bayous near what is now downtown New Orleans. Thanks to a band of enthusiastic collectors in the early years of the twentieth century, many of the plants were transplanted to private and public gardens, ensuring their survival when city development subsequently destroyed their natural habitat.

John K. Small, then Curator of the New York Botanical Gardens, first saw Louisiana irises in the 1920s and fell in love with them when he was traveling by train through southern Louisiana. So impressed was he by their diversity and range of colors that he returned many times in the course of the next decade, photographing, identifying and describing more than 70 different plants which he guessed might be species.

Later analysis showed that many were in fact natural hybrids, but his enthusiasm and the ensuing publicity helped popularize Louisiana irises in American horticultural circles, particularly in the South. It was Small who first described *I. giganticaerulea*, a giant blue of the coastal marshes and, according to Richard A. Goula in *The Louisiana Iris*, perhaps the most spectacular and prolific of the group.

Although numbering only five species, their varying characteristics provide a huge range of possibilities for breeding cultivars to widely differing specifications. The natural hybridization that had occurred before they were "discovered" had already introduced a wider range of color variations than exists in any other iris apart from beardeds. Interest in collecting these natural hybrids increased enor-

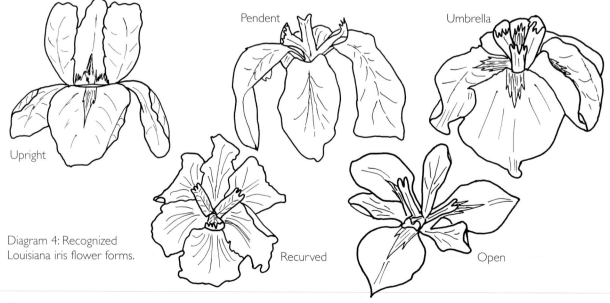

Diagram 4: Recognized Louisiana iris flower forms.

Upright

Pendent

Umbrella

Recurved

Open

Louisiana 'Glowlight'

Louisiana 'Brookvale Overture'

mously with the establishment of the Louisiana Iris Society in 1941, and by the late 1940s controlled hybridizing had begun.

This led to the development of superb cultivars that, according to Graeme Grosvenor in *Iris – Flower of the Rainbow*, have attributes surpassing in both range and quality those of all other iris except bearded. He points out that they contain the genetic make-up to produce short- and tall-growing species, branched and unbranched spikes, straight and zigzag stems, small and large flowers, flared and drooping form, wide and narrow "petals" and large and small rhizomes, as well as their exceptional color range.

So how does the novice iris grower recognize a Louisiana iris? It's not always easy. The form of the flower can vary widely, from slender and drooping to rounded, ruffled and frilly with some hybrids looking not unlike modern Siberian cultivars. Often the standards and the falls overlap each other, so that viewed from above the bloom appears to be composed of two rounded triangles superimposed one on top of the other. Imagine a curvy version of the Star of David. Though colors vary enormously, true fire-engine red has not yet been attained in an iris of any kind but the reddish coloring of *I. fulva* produces cultivars with more definite red than is found in other series of irises.

Overlapping

Semi-double

Ruffled (laced)

Flat (flaring, semi-flaring)

In the 1960s, Joseph K. Mertzweiller of Baton Rouge in Louisiana started working on developing tetraploid cultivars, the first of which were registered in 1973. Called 'Professor Ike' and 'Professor Claude', both these violet irises are excellent garden plants – healthy, vigorous and with abundant foliage. They ushered in a new era in the development of Louisianas. Hybridization continues in the United States, in France and in Australia, where John Taylor developed some exciting new cultivars during the 1990s.

Home gardeners enjoy Louisianas for their tough attitude to life. One grower I know lifted a clump of Louisianas, intending to divide and replant them. But time rushed by and the irises were left out of the ground in a shady area for about six weeks. It wasn't a problem, she reported. Any dead foliage was trimmed off and the rhizomes soaked in a bucket of water. Once they had plumped up a little, they were planted in rich soil and, about two weeks later, new growth appeared.

Culture

Louisianas have three major needs: they must have an adequate supply of water, the soil must be acidic in composition – any soil suitable for camellias and azaleas is fine – and it must be fertile. These three, unlike climate, can largely be controlled by the grower, and Louisiana irises are being successfully grown in widely varying climates, though with a corresponding difference in length of growing season and time of flowering.

The range of zones where they will grow and bloom happily is evident by reports in *The Louisiana Iris* (Caillet and Mertzweiller) from growers across the U.S. Southern Louisiana, the plant's home base, is in hardiness zone 9 where the winters are mild and summers warm. There they start blooming in early spring (mid to late March) and grow for about eight months of the year. In Los Angeles, California, plant hardiness zone 10, where summers are drier than in Louisiana, the growing season is close to 12 months,

Louisiana seed pod.

provided they are watered adequately. The normal blooming period starts in mid-spring (mid to late April).

Surprisingly, these irises will also grow in the cold midwest, plant hardiness zone 4, where the climate could scarcely be more different from that of their natural habitat. There, Louisiana irises survive the frozen winters either insulated by heavy snowfalls or, lacking snow, with the protection of a heavy mulch. They grow for about five months and bloom for a long season in summer, often starting in the second week of June and continuing into July. What a versatile plant! There is some doubt, however, about the cold hardiness of cultivars bred from *I. hexagona*. Generally speaking, the smaller the stature of the iris, the more cold-tolerant it tends to be.

Though Louisianas enjoy warmth and basking in the full sun they will cope happily with half a day's sunshine or all-day filtered light, yet another example of their adaptability.

In areas where summers are very hot they will need some heat protection: mulching is effective, while also conserving moisture and restricting weed growth.

Louisianas like rich, heavy soil and will grow happily in regular beds, at the edge of water, in a bog, in standing water preferably to a depth of not more than 1 in (2 cm), or in pots placed in ponds.

They are also ideal irises to grow as container plants for the patio, as long as they are given adequate water. In spring, when they make rapid growth, and during the flowering season, sit the container in a saucer continually filled with water. They are heavy feeders too, so when potted, they will need frequent fertilizing. Well-rotted animal manures are good. Remove the saucer of water once flowering is over – this imitates its natural habitat, where the swamps often dry out in summer.

One irisarian grows her Louisianas in large buckets standing in a trench about 10 in (25 cm) deep and flooded weekly from early spring until flowering. Her growing medium is a mixture of cow manure, grape waste (crushed skins, seeds and stems from a winery), and compost with an acidic content. Because Louisianas increase quickly they need to be replanted annually when grown in pots. Do it at the beginning of fall and feed them in spring with a weak solution of cow manure.

Remember that the foliage nourishes the plant and during their summer dormancy most Louisianas will grow better if they are kept watered during hot dry spells. In late summer and fall, resist the temptation to pull off dead foliage as this can damage the rhizome increase. Dead leaves will eventually shrivel up and blend into the mulch.

Planting and division

In keeping with their extremely adaptable nature, Louisianas can be moved at any time of the year, but it's usual to plant and divide them straight after flowering, or in the fall. To divide, dig the rhizomes and cut back the foliage to about 8 in (20 cm). Rhizomes should be planted about 1 in (3 cm) deep. When Louisianas are planted or replanted, it's a good idea to allow time for new roots to develop before giving them lots of water. This avoids the risk

of rhizomes rotting in wet soil before their roots are ready to suck up the moisture. It follows that irises planted in pots and intended to be grown in water need about four weeks to develop roots before they are submerged.

These irises tend to increase fast, particularly when submerged, and ideally should be divided every three years as flowering diminishes if the clumps become too cramped.

It is not only the flowers of Louisiana irises that are eye-catching; their seed pods can be huge and add another dimension to the garden, hanging from their stalks like great big green eggs. But they are heavy. If you want to save seed you will need to stake your plants once the seed pods form. Louisiana seeds come with a corky covering that allows them to float and helps to explain their wide dispersal in their swampy homeland.

Once this covering dries out, though, germination is more difficult, so in mild climates seed should be planted immediately once it ripens. In cold climates, however, it should not be planted until spring.

Plant the seeds in pots, in a planting mix that is fertile and porous – a medium of equal parts of sand and well-rotted manure works well. Cover them

'King's Dream', a recent Louisiana bred by John Taylor.

Louisiana 'Italian Affair'

with about ½ in (1 cm) of mix and keep them moist and shaded.

Wait until the seedlings have developed a good root ball before attempting to plant them out. They can be almost root-bound and as tall as 6-8 in (15-20 cm) before there is any need to move them. Expect to see flowers in the second season.

Flower characteristics

As with other irises, the flowers of the species in the group generally have a slender profile. The standards are narrower than the falls and tend to sit upright, although *I. fulva* departs from this form with both the standards and the falls drooping and only the style arms standing erect. But the blooms of many of today's cultivars bear little resemblance to this species' flower form. The diagrams on pages 60-61 show the many forms that Louisiana iris blooms can take and this diversity is one reason why Louisianas are so popular today. There is a shape to please everyone.

Colors range from shades of white through cream and yellow to rich gold. Blues, mauves and purples of all tones abound and there are Louisianas in variations of red, as well as tans, terracotta, brown and chocolate. These darker colors often appeal to floral artists. A true pink has emerged recently and there are true bicolors and tricolors. In contrast to bearded irises, the style arms are an important part in the visible color patterning and form of Louisiana irises, creating a contrast to the main floral parts. Some of the modern rounded cultivars bear standards that have assumed a similar shape and elevation to the falls, and the style arms sit upright, looking like miniature standards.

The size of the blooms ranges from the smallest at about 3 in (8 cm) to the grandeur of flowers that are more than 7 in (18 cm) across, and there are usually between five and seven blooms on each spike.

The signal on the falls in many cultivars is frequently bright yellow or a limy yellow that contrasts with the main color. Where it appears on both the falls and the standards, such as in 'Real Treasure', bred by John Taylor in 1994, the effect is dramatic. On this iris the signals are greenish lemon, finely marked with the purple of the petals; they form a stunning six-pointed star with the style arms emerging in the center as up-curled, frilly pompoms. 'Charlotte's Tutu', bred from a Taylor hybrid by Australian Heather Pryor in 1996, also features six strong signals. 'King's Dream' (Taylor 1997), a wine-red with six bold yellow signals and fine cream-yellow edging on the slightly frilled petals, is typical of the trend in modern hybrids towards large ruffled blooms.

Blooming

Most modern Louisianas carry a terminal spike plus three branches, each of which will produce several flowers (referred to by hybridizers as four flowering points). Depending on the cultivar, each bloom will last two or three days.

With careful planning in the choice of cultivars, it is possible to have Louisianas blooming in the garden for a period of about a month, usually from mid-spring, but in very cold climates it can be early summer.

Species

I. hexagona comes from the southeastern United States, adjacent to the Atlantic coast and the Gulf of Mexico, so it likes warm summers and mild winters. The flowers are a gorgeous blue, sometimes varying towards lavender, with a narrow yellow signal on the falls, and standards that are upright and slim. The branching stems vary in height, from 12-36 in (30-90 cm), and as with all Louisianas, it has sword-like, yellow-green foliage.

I. brevicaulis is another blue-flowered species, generally paler than *I. hexagona*, with an open form. It is the dwarf of the species in this group and it occurs further north than *I. hexagona*, often found in open pasture where moisture is high during the growing season. With much shorter stalks – 10-14 in (25-35 cm) – than its cousins, the flowers are always carried low, never appearing above the foliage. *I. brevicaulis* is quite hardy and in Louisiana flowers in early to mid-May, later than the other species. A notable feature is the stalk, which zigzags at the nodes.

I. giganticaerulea, as the name suggests, is also blue-flowered, though it may vary somewhat through shades of wisteria and lavender to white. Stalks are tall and straight, occasionally growing to 66 in (165 cm). The slender flowers are carried above the foliage, giving the plant an air of elegance, especially when grown in clumps. This is a plant that likes rich soil and thrives in flooded conditions, growing in full sun or partial shade in open swamps.

I. fulva is a robust plant ranging in height from 18-32 in (45-80 cm). It is notable for its dull red, coppery, orange-red, even (rarely) chrome yellow flowers, borne on stems that are almost straight. Both falls and standards are drooping, and the short, semi-erect style arms look like a butterfly sitting atop the bloom. This iris caused a sensation in Britain when it first arrived in 1814 because of its color. It occurs abundantly in Louisiana but has been found as far north as Ohio, growing in partial shade to full sun, in open swamps, in wooded swamps where light is sufficient, and alongside streams and canals. Usual flowering time is early summer and it's one of the easiest to grow.

I. nelsonii was not "discovered" until 1938 and occurs naturally only in a very limited area south of Abbeville in Louisiana. It is a tall-growing plant with stalks that may reach 44 in (110 cm) and are often branched, while the flowers have long reflexed falls and standards, creating a bloom of rather languid appearance. The flower, varying in color from red to a dull terracotta with a hint of lavender, is similar to that of *I. fulva*, and like it, has made it possible for hybridizers to introduce red into their breeding programs. For this reason it is a very important member of the Louisiana family, having contributed to many of the incredibly beautiful modern cultivars.

Other beardless irises

Separate from the groups of beardless irises already described, there are other series containing very few species, or in some cases, merely one species. Some of these are known as garden plants, others are rare in cultivation. A selection follows of the more obtainable ones or those that are easy to cultivate.

I. lactea, after a period of confusing name changes, at present comprises a group of one. Perhaps to compensate for its lonely classification, it occurs in a variety of colors, ranging from blue to purple to dingy gray-blue and sometimes white. Its flower is scented and quite distinctive in shape, almost forming a wide V; its standards are very erect though the falls flare slightly.

Height also varies, with flowering stems of between 6-12 in (15-30 cm), each bearing one or two blooms. Its fibrous rhizomes with long wiry roots help it withstand drought.

Native to Kashmir, Manchuria, northeast China and Korea, it often forms dense clumps on river

I. lactea

banks, by roadsides, sandy lake margins and dry river beds in a huge range of altitudes. The tough, gray-green leaves grow taller than the flowers and, in some countries, are used for making baskets. Known to be salt-resistant, they die down in late winter. In its native habitats *I. lactea* blooms between May and July, depending on altitude. Consistent with its range of living conditions, this is a very hardy iris. Provided with really well-drained soil and a good meal of rotted animal manure or acidic fertilizer in spring and fall, it will grow easily in areas with warm summers. It does not take kindly to being moved, though. If you must divide it, do so as soon as flowering is over and replant it immediately, treating its long roots with tender loving care. It will grow from seed, though it is one of those plants that requires patience – it takes three or more years from germination to flower.

I. foetidissima, native to western Europe and north Africa, naturalized in Britain and regarded as a noxious weed in some countries, is another iris species with a classification all to itself. Its name,

The brilliant seeds of *I. foetidissima*.

meaning "most stinking" iris, refers to the smell given off by the leaves when crushed – certainly not chosen by a graduate with a marketing degree! But how many people go around crushing iris leaves anyway? Could not the person who named it have concentrated on some aspect of the flowers? Well, no. They don't stink noticeably but they are small, uninteresting and a dull mustard color. Unlike most iris flowers you would walk past them without a second glance. So why didn't the christening authority focus on the seeds? For this iris is a show-stopper when the pods twist and split open in late fall to display ranks of startling red seeds. They hang onto the stalk through winter and are very attractive for indoor floral arrangements. As a plant *I. foetidissima* can be useful, flourishing as it does in damp shady corners. But take care to collect its seeds before they drop for it can become invasive.

Some clear yellow and violet cultivars are worth growing for their flowers and there is a variegated form which is useful in the garden though it does not set seed readily.

Longipetala irises

Known also as Rocky Mountain irises, it is not hard to guess that these two species originate in North America, though they are not only found in the Rocky Mountains. A cool climate, wet winters, and dry summers are to their liking.

I. longipetala is found in coastal areas of California. The slender-petaled flower has an ethereal quality to it and is palest lavender or nearly white with long falls, wavy at the edge and clearly inscribed with symmetrical lilac veining radiating out from a faint yellow signal. The standards are darker, the veining smudgily marked.

It is a hardy and relatively undemanding plant, likes loose soil and perfect drainage, basks in full sun and requires plenty of water during its growing season, preferring to dry off after flowering. The evergreen foliage grows to about 2 ft (60 cm), and flower spikes may reach 3 ft (90 cm), each carrying up to eight flowers.

This is an iris to grow from seed if you can wait two years for the flowers to appear. If you are impatient, propagate by division immediately after it flowers, and before summer dryness checks its growth.

I. missouriensis is found in the high country of the Rocky Mountains up to 10,000 ft (3000 m), as well as in meadows, along stream banks and in scrub or pine forest in western North America from Mexico to British Columbia.

Common in inland California, especially east of the Sierra Nevada, it is similar in appearance to *I. longipetala* but the plant is sturdier, carries fewer flowers and is less easily cultivated. It is also much more variable, sometimes appearing in pale blue or clothed in mauve and white, with stems ranging in height from 8-20 in (20-50 cm). Foliage is gray-green and dormant in winter. It also requires plenty of rain up to flowering time, followed by dry summers.

I. missouriensis

Tripetala irises

This is another small group of species and only one, *I. setosa*, is found commonly in cultivation. The name refers to the fact that at first glance these flowers appear to have only three petals because the standards are so small, reduced sometimes to bristle-like proportions, and much smaller than the style arms.

I. setosa in the wild is widely distributed over many cold, wet northern hemisphere regions, from eastern Asia, through Japan to Alaska and the east coast of Canada. Its form therefore is extremely variable. It may reach only 6 in (15 cm) in one place while attaining 3 ft (90 cm) elsewhere. Wet meadows, peaty bogs, light woods and shorelines are where it feels at home, but it is an easy-to-grow garden plant, in appearance rather similar to Siberian irises, although unlike them, it tends to be short-lived.

It likes a moist acidic soil in sun or semi-shade and the branched stems bear six or more flowers in early summer. They are usually blue to purple and the blade of the falls is very wide, which gives the bloom a generous spreading appearance. The tall forms look graceful beside water, though they make good border plants too, especially in combination with lighter colored variegated grasses of a similar height. Smaller forms are great for rock gardens.

It is another of those irises with foliage stained red at the base. Rhizomes are fleshy and frequently covered with fiber from the remains of dead leaves –

perhaps this is insulation for its cold natural environment.

Named cultivars include 'Kosho-en' with white flowers and 'Kirigamine' with rich velvety blue-purple flowers.

I. tridentata (syn *I. tripetala*) likes similar conditions to *I. setosa* and is a good iris to grow in a container in water, as long as the rhizome is above water level.

I. prismatica 'Alba'

Below: *I. setosa* 'Arctica'

I. prismatica is another lonely species, the only one of its kind and not commonly grown. Native to North America, where it is found in damp woodlands and marshy ground along the Atlantic coast from Nova Scotia to Carolina, it grows in tufts of thin glaucous leaves and likes moist soil and light shade. It has dainty, light violet flowers and grows to 2 ft (60 cm) with a slender wiry stem. There is a white form, *I. prismatica* 'Alba'.

I. unguicularis (syn. *I. stylosa*) really begs to be planted in carpets – or lacking that kind of space, you may have to settle for a few doormats. It is native to stony places in Algeria, Crete, Greece, Syria and Asia Minor.

Flowering begins spasmodically in the fall, continuing through winter and romps into spring if it's happy. The flower has virtually no stem, just a perianth tube that grows about 8 in (20 cm) above the ground. To show them in all their beauty, it is a good idea to cut back the leaves at the beginning of winter to allow the flowers to unfold undamaged, as the foliage grows to about 24 in (60 cm). They come in every shade of blue from pale to deep sky-blue; some are mauve-violet, and there is also a white form *I. unguicularis* 'Alba', as well as a soft pink flowered variety, 'Starkers Pink'. It blooms later than the species and is smaller, with finer leaves, though the flowers have broad falls and standards.

I like the description of a planting of this tiny early flowering iris from Russell Page, an English designer who made gardens for the rich and famous. Asked to rehabilitate a garden in France in which there were 18 acres (7 hectares) of neglected olive trees, he tore out all the miscellaneous under-planting and then planted hundreds of *I. unguicularis* among rough grass, interspersed with hundreds of common cream freesias and occasional groups of *I. wattii*. Imagine the perfume of an evening! And, as he explained, the low plants allowed the gnarled gray trunks of the olive trees to be seen in all their character.

Author Alison Nicoll has a thriving clump of these irises growing beneath a large *Cupressus macrocarpa* hedge that provides shelter for her extensive beds of bearded irises. They start flowering after the first rains of fall (which slugs and snails well know, so it is a good idea to spread slug pellets around) and she grooms them from time to time by raking out the dead foliage with her fingers.

I. unguicularis likes well-drained soil, benefits from an occasional dressing of lime, needs sunny conditions but is cold-hardy and frost-resistant. Plant it out in spring and water it frequently until it is well-established. In fact it needs ample water throughout the year, except in summer when it prefers to sunbathe.

This is an easy-care species that doesn't need to be divided regularly to maintain its flowering and if you must divide clumps, make sure the divisions are not too small as they re-establish grudgingly. Left to its own devices it will re-seed easily. Where parent plants are affected by a virus, seedlings will be free of contamination. This is a plant to cherish, both for its perfume and its early flowering habit.

I. lazica resembles *I. unguicularis* but is adapted to more humid, damper areas and can tolerate cooler temperatures. A native of northeastern Turkey and Georgia, it grows on shady sandy banks, often beneath scrub or bracken. Its flowers are somewhat somber – deep purple-blue with large upright standards and pendent falls – and, unlike *I. unguicularis*, have no perfume. In mild climates it flowers in winter, but where winters are cold, it waits until early spring.

CHAPTER 5

Bulbous Irises

While the word rhizome may fall into the category of unusual gardening terminology to some, most people are familiar with the term bulbs. What could be more common than an onion bulb?

The irises in this division grow from bulbs similar in make-up to the vegetable that causes so much grief when it's peeled. Whether we are aware of it or not, some of the best-known irises – those most often seen in florists' shops – grow from bulbs, the Dutch, English and Spanish irises, tall aristocrats with shapely, rich-colored, purple-blue and yellow blooms.

All the bulbous irises lose their leaves after flowering, all are summer dormant and need to be lifted from time to time, and all the species can be raised from seed, though the wait for the first flower will be longer than with seed-raised plants of the rhizome-forming groups. Increase of hybrids true to form can come only from bulblets that form each season from the parent bulb and of course species also increase this way.

As with daffodils, the foliage of these irises starts to look untidy once flowering is over for the season. When the leaves start to flop around, tidy gardeners have that urge to grab the secateurs and cut them off. But don't. The bulb is pregnant. It needs cherishing and the leaves help to nourish it. The last month or two of growth is vitally important, for this is when the buds for the following season are forming.

Opposite: Spanish iris 'Solfatere', blue flowers with yellow blotch, and yellow-flowered 'Fredricka'.

Dutch iris 'Professor Blaauw'

Bulbous irises do not like heavy clay but adding sand, gravel and humus can turn this kind of soil into a hospitable home. When storing the bulbs out of the ground, make sure their resting place is shaded, cool and dry, and that air circulation is good.

Xiphium – Dutch, English and Spanish irises

When you buy irises as cut flowers you will most likely buy Dutch, English or Spanish irises. But the names are confusing. The ones we buy and grow are mostly hybrids bred from an original group of about eight species, all from western Europe and north Africa and hardy to zone 9. The English irises are hybrids derived from *I. latifolia*, a native of the Pyrenees; Spanish irises are descended from *I.*

xiphium, which originated in countries bordering the Mediterranean, including Spain; the Dutch irises were developed early last century by Dutch growers seeking to extend the flowering season of the Spanish iris by crossing it with *I. xiphium* species and *I. tingitana* from Morocco. The Dutch hybrids produce bigger, earlier-blooming flowers than the true Spanish irises. Now their cultivation is so controlled that flowers can be produced at any time of the year – hence their huge commercial sales.

Each bulb most commonly bears one flowering stem which produces two blooms that open in succession. Dutch irises flower in spring, before the Tall Beardeds but at the same time as many of the Spanish irises. Both should be lifted at least every two or three years, just when the foliage is drying off, and left to dry in a shady place. But they must be replanted in time for the new roots to grow – about August in the northern hemisphere, February in the southern hemisphere. Left out of the ground until fall, the bulbs will lose vitality, be more susceptible to disease, and their flowers will be of poorer quality.

They like good drainage, moderately rich, well-worked soil in a sunny location, and a light top-dressing of lime. Poor soil makes small flowers; too rich a soil may encourage fungal disease. Plant the bulbs about 4 in (10 cm) deep.

Xiphium hybrids are tall plants, some growing to 3 ft (1 m) or more in height. The only way for them to reproduce true to form is from the bulblets that grow on the parent bulb each season once flowering is finished. If the main bulb is lifted every year and the babies detached, it is possible to build stock quickly.

Lift the bulb in early summer and allow it about a month to dry thoroughly before detaching the small bulblets. Put these back in the earth as quickly as possible before there is a chance for mold to attack them. Soil rich in humus will encourage them to continue growing until late in the season.

Spanish 'Delft's Blue', a dark purple-blue hybrid,

the paler blue 'Enchantress', the pale blue, early flowering Dutch 'Wedgwood' and the darker blue 'Professor Blaauw' are rewarding plants for the garden and they make excellent cut flowers. When cutting blooms, always leave at least four leaves to nourish the bulb and take care not to damage it with the knife or secateurs.

Xiphiums are prone to virus attack. This shows as yellow streaking in the leaves which then rot at the base. Infected bulbs need to be dug out and burned. Fumigate the ground before replanting with any bulbs.

Species

I. xiphium, giving its name to the group, has several color forms in the wild – two-toned blues, yellows and combinations of whites, yellows and blues. The signal, whether a stripe or patch, is gold or yellow and is often quite prominent. The foliage, which appears in the fall, is glaucous and initially fine, gradually broadening as it matures.

I. tingitana is a stunning plant. The tall, silvery, broad foliage is lovely in winter and the flowers are gorgeous, not because of any flamboyance but for their classic style that never loses its appeal. The standards are lavender blue, long and upright, tapering to a point. The falls are pendent, very blue on the wavy margins but shading out to palest lavender on the blades with clear yellow signals. Growing to over 3 ft (1 m), it bears only one flowering spike.

Plant the bulb about $1^1/_2$ in (5 cm) deep with sand above and below. It likes a loose soil rich in humus, good drainage, a hot sunny position and protection from frost. It appreciates lime and a top-dressing of potash in the growing season, during winter and early spring. In climates with summer rain it should be lifted after the foliage has died down and replanted in early fall. But it's a temperamental creature. You can give it all this care and still find it will not flower reliably!

Xiphium hybrids 'Delft's Blue' and the paler blue 'Enchantress'.

I. juncea is notable for its vivid orange-yellow blooms, the second one in the sheath rising above the first on a long pedicel tube. They come into bloom at the same time as the Tall Beardeds. A more slender plant than the Dutch hybrids, it grows to about 12 in (30 cm) with the flowers produced on 30 in (75 cm) stems. The bulbs differ from other bulbous irises with a hard, dark brown skin that splits into long fibers at the neck. Usually this plant increases by producing two large bulbs from the base but it can be grown from seed in sandy soil.

I. latifolia (syn. *I. xiphioides*) is the latest-flowering of the Xiphium group, coming into bloom in early summer at the same time as Japanese irises. A native of damp meadows in the Pyrenees, it is used to snow in winter, and thawing snow and rain in spring and fall, so it does not need to dry out in summer, though it never likes to be waterlogged. It also tolerates lightly filtered shade.

Foliage, similar to that of Juno irises (see below), first appears in spring. The flowers, ranging in color through all the purple-lavender-blue shades to white, are borne on 12 in (30 cm) stems. These plants are better left undisturbed for three or four years; when finally lifted after the foliage has died down, the separate bulbs should be replanted immediately, as each develops an important root system during summer and fall.

Juno irises

Imagine a plant with foliage that grows up the stem in alternating steps, rather like young leeks or corn, and you will have a picture in your mind of what Juno irises look like. In fact, their appearance is so different from other irises, there is talk of classifying them in a genus all their own. But as that has not yet happened we will still consider them part of the iris family. It is a large group, comprising over 50 species, but few of them are commonly grown. They are natives of arid regions with extremes of climate in central Asia and around the Mediterranean. As you would expect from their native habitats, they are frost-hardy (to 10°F/–12°C). The flowers, of unusual form, grow out of the leaf axils with standards unrecognizable as such. Either they are horizontal or they point downwards like stiff little wings, while the style arms appear to take the normal position of standards. The falls may be horizontal or held upright at an angle of about 45 degrees. When cutting Junos for indoors, take as few leaves as possible to avoid weakening the bulb.

Junos have thick-necked bulbs clad in thin brown tissue with fleshy white roots – like long radishes – that extend down and out into the ground. These roots are replaced each year so that an undamaged bulb, when it is dug up, will reveal both old and new sets at the same time. Handle the bulbs with care as the new storage roots are brittle and precious. In the fall the fleshy roots send out another set of roots, fibrous in texture, which start the annual growth cycle.

These irises are easy to grow so long as a few main points are kept in mind. Excellent drainage is very important. A raised bed in full sun, filled with a mixture of half sand and half soil, is ideal. They are suitable plants for containers as they don't like being disturbed. In theory, they are supposed to be kept quite dry during summer dormancy, and in pots it is easy to move them under cover once flowering is finished.

However, one grower reports that this may not be as necessary as has been supposed. For years she had always gone to great pains to protect her Junos in summer, making sure no moisture came near them. But recently, during the wettest summer for a long time, they were exposed to large amounts of rain and showed no ill effects the following spring. Superb drainage probably helped.

They relish a top-dressing of lime and blood meal or well-rotted animal manure in the fall.

Because the plants are often hard to source, it may be necessary to grow Junos from seed. They take about four years to flower.

I. bucharica

Species

I. bucharica is probably the best-known of the Junos. It will grow up to 20 in (50 cm) but is usually smaller. Rather like the blooms of gladioli, flowers open from the top down, with large bulbs producing as many as eight in succession. Standards and falls are creamy yellow and the broad upright crests are white, as are the style arms. It flowers about the middle of spring.

I. persica comes from Iran and Turkey and flowers almost at ground level in late winter and spring with a wide variation of color in its flowers – greenish blue, white, yellow, red-purple or violet. Although it has been cultivated for centuries it is not widely grown or easily available.

It is, however, important as one of the parents, with *I. aucheri* (syn *I. sindjarensis*), of *I.* 'Sindpers', which is a vigorous grower and has flowers of a lovely cool hue between slate-green, pale turquoise and gray. Growing to about 4 in (10 cm) high, it flowers early in winter.

I. magnifica is robust and one of the more commonly grown Junos, good for a sunny rock garden. Look for it in specialist nurseries. It is a taller species, growing between 12-24 in (30-60 cm) high, with flowers in pale lilac and yellow. Wide wings feature on the haft of the falls that act as drainage channels to take moisture away from the ovaries.

I. warleyensis, from Bukhara in Uzbekistan, is hardy, bears narrow foliage and has attractive flowers of lilac, with a sharply defined pattern on the falls of white, dark purple and yellow.

I. willmottiana is a robust, short plant 6-10 in (15-25 cm) high and at flowering time the stem is packed with about eight broad, shiny leaves which gradually elongate.

The flowers are soft lavender or pale purple with deeper lavender and white on the falls. It also bears the drainage wings on the falls that are a feature of some of these irises.

I. cycloglossa is one of the easier Junos to grow. Its flowers, appearing late in the season, are rather like the shape of Xiphium blooms with large erect standards. They are perfumed with the scent of cloves and are a bright purple-blue. It is usually described as having one to a few branches, each bearing one or two flowers, but one grower recently reported 10 flowers on her plant! Well worth the four-year wait from seed to bloom.

Reticulata or dwarf bulbous irises

There's really nothing to compare with the first signs of spring after months of cold, gray winter dormancy. But if you can't wait that long, then grow Reticulata irises – and spare a moment's sympathy for those who garden in lush sub-tropical climates and can't grow them easily. These tiny members of the iris family are perfect for cold climates (zone 5). Just when you despair of winter ever lifting, they arrive with a hint of spring long before the weather follows suit. The species *I. histrioides* actually pops through bare earth in mid-winter. It's followed a few weeks later by *I. reticulata*, which gives its name to the series, reflecting the net-like coat of fibers protecting the bulb. (Reticulum means net in Latin.)

Below: *I. warleyensis* Below right: *I. histrioides*

The foliage in all but one species is also distinctive, being square in cross section, while the tiny flowers resemble miniature Spanish irises.

Like many of their relations, they come from Russia and the Middle East where they thrive in cold winters and hot dry summers. Probably there are myriad species still to be "discovered" in remote areas of Iraq, Iran or Afghanistan.

They are plants for full sun at the edge of a path, or in the rock garden where it's easier to prevent them from being swamped by larger, summer-flowering plants. Give them gritty, reasonably rich, very well-drained soil that is neutral to alkaline. If you grow them in pots, make sure they are fed extra-well.

A good tonic is a quarter of a bucket of chicken manure topped up with water. Serve the Reticulatas a drink of the liquid every two weeks from mid-fall.

For maximum effect, grow these irises in groups and clumps. However, they do need to be lifted every two or three years as they increase quickly when happy, and overcrowding can make them more susceptible to ink disease, a fungus that is sometimes a problem. If necessary, the disease can be controlled by dipping the bulbs in a fungicide prior to planting.

While they like moisture in early summer when the bulbs are in reproductive mode, they don't like lots of summer rain. If this is typical of your climate, they should be lifted annually, once they are dormant – no later than June. It's important to give them plenty of time to develop their root system during fall, so plant them again in mid- to late summer, about 3 in (8 cm) deep, and add a little slow-release fertilizer. Make sure they are well-watered in winter and spring; in heavy soil provide the bulbs with a layer of sand below and above planting level.

If you don't know any gardeners who can pass on some bulbs, the place to look for them is in specialist nurseries or nurseries that stock a range of alpine plants.

I. reticulata

Species

I. reticulata comes from the Caucasus. It is the tallest of the species, with comparatively large flowers sitting about 6-7 in (18-20 cm) above the ground amid the foliage. These flowers are valued for their clear colors – shades of purple striped with gold – and for their perfume, as well as their early spring appearance. And if you can wait three or four years until it flowers, the plant is easy to grow from seed, although it does produce bulblets that mature quickly to flowering stage.

I. reticulata would seem suited for growing in pots or troughs for the flowering to be enjoyed at close quarters. It is easy to move out of view too, when the foliage becomes unsightly. If this works for you, great, but some gardeners find these irises don't thrive in containers. In any case, they should be replanted in the garden after one year in a container and fresh bulbs used in the pots or troughs the following year. You probably have to be fairly dedicated to grow them this way!

I. histrioides has lovely formal, almost navy blue flowers, made spectacular by soft dottings of deeper blue around the white haft with its clear yellow median stripe. They appear long before the foliage and subsequent blooms appear lighter in color, almost a Wedgwood blue. So hardy, it will pierce blankets of snow to display its dainty flowers. Let it naturalize with snowdrops around it.

A miniature species is **I. danfordiae**, bright, showy and yellow – if you're lucky enough to entice it to bloom. It requires rich, light soil and excellent drainage. This one really requires patience even if it does flower for you, for the parent bulb then proceeds to split into infant bulblets that take another three to four years before flowering.

Rather rare is **I. bakeriana**, with slender eight-sided leaves – an unusual but useful identifying feature. Another iris to lift its flower above bare earth, its tiny blooms – 2 in high on 4 in perianth tubes (5 cm x 10 cm) – are light blue with distinctive dark purple splashes on the falls. Bulbs are more pointed and slender than other Reticulatas and it likes sandy soil. Growing this one in a container helps you to keep track of the bulbs and their offsets. Sink it in the ground at planting time to do its growing and bring it inside where you can revel in its gorgeous blooms. Flowering time is after *I. histrioides* and before *I. reticulata*.

I. winogradowii comes from the Caucasus where it grows in damp meadows. Not widely grown, its flowers resemble those of *I. histrioides* but are pale primrose yellow, with darker dotting on the falls. It grows well in semi-shade in peaty, cool soil where summers are dry.

Several cultivars have come onto the market in recent years, all making attractive early spring-flowering garden plants. 'Cantab' is a selected form of *I. reticulata* with pale blue flowers; 'Katharine Hodgkin' has flowers of sea-green, sulfur yellow and blue; 'Sheila Ann Germany' has silver-gray flowers in early spring and a shape that shows her parentage from *I. histrioides*, and 'Natascha' is ivory white with green veins and a yellow blotch.

Below: *I. bakeriana*

CHAPTER 6

Landscaping with Irises

With careful selection, gardeners in a true temperate climate can have irises blooming for 11 months of the year. Realistically, though, only the most dedicated collectors will strive for this. More often gardeners will fall in love with an iris – probably a bearded variety – and then find themselves seduced by a beautiful Siberian, or maybe a tall water-loving Japanese and decide to incorporate a variety of irises into their landscape. From tiny to tall there is one for every situation. But before rushing out to buy your latest love, it makes sense to assess your garden and the needs of your chosen plants. Sun and shade, frost and shelter, soil content and available space are all factors to consider. Think also about color, for in this respect irises are a very obliging design tool. The choice is almost limitless. The range of blues alone is enormous and there is no better color to work with in a garden. It can link the garish with the subtle, softening the one and enhancing the other. Threaded through a garden it adds unity. Dark blues and purples recede; clear blues are more prominent, especially when viewed from a distance.

In the border

If tall is what you need, irises offer lots of possibilities. Tall Beardeds, planted in a bed of their own, look superb in spring in full bloom. But when the flowers fade, the foliage alone looks rather sad and few gardeners today have the space to devote solely to one kind of plant. However, Tall and

Opposite: Tall Bearded irises are gorgeous among spring-flowering shrubs.

Giant gunnera leaves complement the slender form of the Siberian iris.

Intermediate Beardeds look great mixed with perennials. Group them in colors to create impact – a spotty scattering of single plants will not do them justice. Blend several shades of the same color or look for contrasts with flowers that bloom at the same time. Russell lupins, pinks, delphiniums, poppies, honesty, the tall cerise-flowered *Geranium maderense*, columbines, foxgloves and forget-me-nots are some of those with similar flowering times and requirements to bearded irises. After the flowers have gone the leaves remain to make effective textural shapes among bushier plants.

There is a certain satisfaction about putting old varieties of different plants together, as if providing companions from a bygone era. The venerable *I.*

pallida looks stunning beside crimson rugosa roses such as 'Roseraie de L'Hay', 'Scabrosa' or *Rosa rugosa rubra*. Another interesting way to grow old varieties of Tall Beardeds is in a border backed by a hedge of stoechas lavender, which will flower for a long period in spring and again in summer if it is lightly trimmed after the first flush.

Even taller than the Tall Beardeds, and flowering at a similar time, are the hybrid Spurias. Their often strong color make them effective flowers for the back of the border or with a dark green hedge at their backs.

Siberians come in a range of heights. They are easy to grow, and as they bloom in early summer when roses are starting their first flush, these also fit well in a garden of perennials. Their attractive clumping form and tall slender flower stems add definition among fuzzier plants.

Suited to mass planting, they hold their own against weeds in an open area or along a winding walkway. They complement candelabra primulas, and they make an informal planting partnered with

Japanese 'Yoshinga-no-gata' (pale) and 'Good Omen' (dark).

taller variegated grasses, a good background for summer perennials. Late-flowering sedums planted close by, such as *Sedum spectabile* 'Autumn Joy', would take attention away from the dying Siberian foliage in the fall.

Louisiana irises are another tall option, though recent breeding has produced plants of compact size that will fit into any garden scheme, large or small. They are adaptable plants, fitting into a perennial border, a bog garden or potted – in or out of water – as long as water is plentiful during the growing and blooming seasons.

I have seen Louisianas thriving as a border planting alongside a steep drive in a climate with abundant rain in spring and early summer. The run-off from the main road above the driveway provided the irises with plenty of moisture and they rarely needed extra irrigation. Louisianas seem more tolerant of alkalinity than other water irises, and any

lime leaching out from the concrete driveway was apparently harmless.

These irises are slow to come into bloom. The flower spike emerges from the foliage and may take three weeks before the bud finally opens. And though it is the flower that draws the oohs and aahs, remember the part that form plays in any overall design. Stately iris branches, with their slim sheathed buds, add an element of expectation in a garden scene.

Louisianas grow not only where it is too warm for beardeds but will also grow in the same climate.

In bog or water

Water-loving irises can pose problems in mixed borders because of a thirsty habit which may not suit their neighbors. But they are beautiful creatures – in the "must-have" category. One solution is to create a bog garden where they can feel at home with other water-loving plants. Dig out an area of soil the desired shape to a depth of at least 12 in (30 cm). Line the depression with heavy-grade poly-

Stately Siberian irises enhance a water setting.

ethylene and pierce it at intervals to provide drainage. Then refill the area with a slightly acidic, moisture-retentive soil mix – adding pine needles, peat or leaf mold will help – and keep it lower than the surrounding garden for ease of flooding. Rodgersias, hostas, filipendula and gunnera all like moist positions and provide a foil for narrow-leafed irises, whether their flowers be slender classic beauties or flamboyant floozies. Huge gunnera leaves are a wonderful counterpoint to flag irises in a stream area, and lady's mantle is another attractive companion plant, but it should be planted with its feet out of water.

In their country of origin, Japanese irises are planted in public gardens laced with zigzagging boardwalks. The beds are flooded in some areas so even the reflections of the blooms can be admired.

If you have a stream or pool, plant these irises, or Louisianas, alongside the water in clumps of varying tones that blend and harmonize, and create subtle

I. pseudacorus

ribbons of color that delight the eye and beg you to wander among them. And if you don't have a stream, even one clump in a prominent place can add panache to the early summer garden.

In containers

If you don't have a water feature, don't despair. Japanese irises grow successfully in containers and coordinating the pot to complement the flower color or garden furniture is part of the fun. Gardeners with a tiny garden and ample sun but no hint of water can enjoy Japanese irises this way. Place specimen clumps beside a bird bath or a seat where, even without flowers, the foliage will be attractive from spring to late fall. They will thrive with appropriate care, and they can be moved around to change landscaping effects – especially important in a small garden. Choose a large pot, provide lots of water from spring until late summer and feed the plant regularly until the buds form. Then stop, as too much food at this stage may make the buds fall off. Repot the plant after two years. In cold climates

Japanese irises grown in a container are ideal for small gardens.

mulch it in winter or bury the pot in the garden.

Tall irises make a simple but effective focus where the emphasis is on hard landscaping. The boldness of sword-shaped foliage and shapely flower forms seem to be enhanced by the contrast of rocks, gravel and minimal planting.

As an accent plant for a courtyard grow Louisiana irises in a container. They like company, so choose a pot big enough to hold at least three and make sure the plants have plenty of water in spring and summer. Select a variety with dramatic flowers and while they are in bloom, move the pot to a prominent place. Once the flowers have died and the glamor has faded, shift the pot to an insignificant corner where it can be quietly left to its own devices until the following spring. At some stage before the next season, the irises will need to be removed from their pot, divided and repotted as they increase quickly.

I. graminea complements a group of stoechas lavenders.

While Siberians, Tall Beardeds and Spurias are not suited to container growing, most other irises will live in pots. It's an easy way to provide them with a growing medium to suit their individual needs. Whatever the iris, it will need regular fertilizing as they tend to be heavy feeders and will quickly exhaust any nutrients available in the potting mix.

In the rock garden

Tall irises hold their own in the hurly burly of border life, but small varieties can be quickly overpowered in similar conditions. For them, a rock garden is perfect. With the level raised, drainage is good; pockets can be filled with soil to suit the individual needs of a host of small plants, including irises. It's the ideal situation for early-flowering Miniature Dwarf Beardeds. I lived once where great hunks of schist were part of the landscape. I filled up depressions in the rocks with soil and planted Dwarf Bearded irises. They enjoyed the alkaline conditions and excellent drainage, made lovely hummocks of color in early spring and survived the hot dry summers – though not without some stress.

Plant *I. cristata* in front of Dwarf Beardeds, preferably close to a pathway where passersby can admire the flowers, and place the taller *I. graminea* and Pacific Coast hybrids at the back where they can form spreading clumps.

Clumps of Reticulatas also enjoy a rock garden, with small hebes or dwarf rhododendrons in the background. Scabiosa, rock cress, dwarf phlox, alyssum and aubretia are companion plants to contribute color – just make sure they don't swamp the rhizomes of the bearded irises. Bulbous irises of the Juno varieties, also suited to rock garden culture, will cope with groundcovers and come through mats of foliage.

CHAPTER 7

Picking and Packing

The intricate form of the flower and their incredible range of colors make irises highly desirable cut flowers. There is an iris to match any decor and massed in a vase they make an awesome display.

I recently took a lovely bunch of Intermediate Beardeds for the front desk of the office where I work. "Are they bearded iris?" asked my colleagues. "What a pity," one replied when I said yes. "They won't last very long."

"Just you wait and see," I reassured them. I had taken the flowers in bud and the vase lasted a full week, with several blooms still out the following Monday.

The flowers are undoubtedly fragile – even getting the blooms from the garden to the house becomes an issue the minute you cut a stem. But to get long-lasting results, pick a stem when the first flower is nearly open and the second bud down is showing some color. Then all the lower buds will gradually open in succession.

Of course as the flowers open and finish they should be removed and another bud behind the first flower will be revealed. Stems that have seven or more buds will easily last a week in a vase. If you choose a stem where the second buds are the only ones left, the flowers will last no more than three days.

Pick irises in the cool of early morning or late evening. Choose spikes where the first bloom is almost open and lay it carefully in a flat container.

Opposite and right: Dutch irises make excellent cut flowers.

Several spikes can be laid together, arranged so the buds don't touch each other. Ensure that there is no moisture on the leaves or flowers. If possible, before traveling or arranging the flowers in a vase, keep the freshly cut stems standing in cool water in a temperature-controlled "cool room" overnight. This will slow down the opening of the buds, reduce transpiration and strengthen the stems.

Bearded irises lend themselves to vase life because of their multiple branches and blooms, but Spuria irises also make superb cut flowers. With strong stems, they give height to the back of a display. They carry multi-budded spikes and the flowers last well in water as do the blooms of Dutch, English and Spanish irises, the varieties most widely used as cut flowers.

Modern hybrid Japanese irises and Louisianas, with their wide rounded blooms, look spectacular in a vase. One bloom complemented with a few leaves is all it takes to make a sophisticated arrangement.

Have flowers, will travel

With a little care, getting your blooms home from the florist, exhibiting flowers or taking them anywhere by car, bus, train or plane can be done successfully. When it is in full bloom with more than one flower out, transporting a stem of bearded iris can be risky. Attempting to move several stems in flower is a real challenge. If the flowers touch each other they are likely to momentarily catch and tear one or both blooms and it's incredibly easy to dislodge the flowers from their sockets, spoiling a well-balanced spike.

Getting in and out of cars is often where the damage occurs. Naturally it is much easier to transport the stems when the fragile flowers are not fully out. To delay them opening, keep the spikes cool.

Plan your journey. Ensure there are facilities at your destination to place all the blooms in water as soon as you arrive; allow enough space for them to open, as many will, overnight; and prepare a box about 4-6 in (10-15 cm) deep, long enough to take the length of the stems. It will need a lid. A polystyrene box will protect the stems from external heat and ice packs can be added to keep the temperature down.

For a shorter journey a cardboard box will suffice. Several stems can be accommodated in a box this size. Line the box with newspaper and allow a good amount to fold over, enclosing all the stems. Dry, non-chemically treated tissue paper can be wrapped around any blooms that look likely to open too soon and some that may have already opened may be persuaded to close and hold that way with tissue. A marker pen is needed to label the stems if they are being exhibited at a show.

Siberians are beautiful in the garden or as cut flowers. 'Summer Skies', pale blue; 'Fisherman's Morning', purple; 'My Love', dark blue.

Dry the cooled stems (the box contents must not be at all damp), wrap any buds that show signs of opening immediately and lay each stem in the box, staggering the stems so the buds don't touch each other. Place layers of paper between each layer of stems. Continue packing with the objective being to avoid any movement of the spikes during the journey. When the box is full, fold the extra paper over the top, add any ice packs outside the newspaper, not touching any stems, and seal the box. Carried like this, irises should survive well for up to 24 hours.

At the other end of the journey, lift the stems carefully from the box – flowers wrapped in tissue may open as soon as this is removed – and place them in water. If the irises are for showing, it's best to unpack the morning before the show, allowing, if possible, 12-24 hours before judging. This gives time for further blooms to open and expand fully. In a cold place, if you wish to hasten the opening, have the heaters on overnight; to encourage a particular bloom, I have used a hair blow-dryer, but care is needed not to get too close.

CHAPTER 8

Pests and Diseases

Clean gardening practices are the best defence against disease but particularly so with bearded irises. As with people, where careful hygiene is observed and the right amounts of food and water are provided, disease is much less likely to strike. It makes sense to keep plants weed-free and tidy up dead foliage where snails and slugs love to lurk.

Japanese irises are resistant to rhizome rot and fungal or viral diseases and, along with Siberians, are the healthiest of all irises. But when a fungus does attack Siberians, part of the clump dies off. Dig it up, cut away and burn the affected part and soak the remainder in a fungicide solution. If possible, replant it in fresh soil and water it in with the solution. Poor drainage can be the cause.

Californian irises are often similarly affected and, to prevent the disease, dip the plants in fungicide and water them well with the solution. If it's a real problem the bed may need fumigating.

The leaves of bearded irises have a waxy surface that gives the plant some protection from both pests and diseases. However, this also means that sprays won't stick and their potency can be lost. It is wise to add a spreader to any spray to achieve maximum effect.

Leaf spot: Humidity and cool nights followed by warm days are conditions conducive to leaf spot. It is caused by a fungus and indicated by multiple small brown spots with yellowish margins on the leaves. It is most likely to affect bearded irises and Louisianas so try to choose disease-resistant cultivars. If you make sure they receive adequate water in spring, delivered preferably to their roots

Siberian 'Ruby Wine'. Siberians are among the healthiest of all irises.

and not by an overhead system, leaf spot should not be a major problem. If it does occur, cleanly trim back to unaffected leaves and spray with a suitable fungicide and add a spreader such as dish detergent.

Bacterial disease: This is recognized by brown streaking of the leaves and yellowing of the tips. The disease will quickly travel down the leaf and may be followed by rhizome rot. Treat as for leaf spot.

Japanese iris, the perfect plant beside water.

Rust: This disease affects mainly Louisianas and bearded irises. Try to choose resistant varieties. Indicated by multiple tiny reddish brown spots that appear "rusty" when touched, it usually begins at the tip of the leaf and then extends downwards. The spots occur during cool dry weather. Sprays are available for rust but infected leaves should be cut back to healthy foliage and the diseased leaves burned.

Rhizome rot: Also known as soft rot. The rhizome itself becomes soft, mushy and smelly and the plant will collapse very quickly. If you diagnose this in time, the plant may be saved by lifting the rhizome and cutting away all the soft parts. Dry in the sun, then drench the fresh cut with 50/50 bleach and water or dust with flowers of sulfur.

Soft rot may be prevented by reducing the supply of nitrogen. A slow-release fertilizer at planting time may also help to reduce its incidence. It tends to be more prevalent in wet and humid weather and can result from poor drainage.

Viral diseases: Indicated by yellow streaking in the leaves. It is not often a major problem with bearded irises, but if severe it is wise to destroy the plant.

Divisions from a badly affected plant will carry the disease with them. Spray if there is an attack of aphids, as they may spread this disease.

Pests: These vary according to country, climate and conditions. Rhizome borer is probably the most serious and it occurs in the eastern and midwestern states of the U.S. Young larvae attack the foliage, working down from the tips. Damage appears as pinholes and notches eaten out of the foliage. One larva eventually arrives at the base and starts munching its way through one or more rhizomes. The whole fan may collapse. Control is best achieved by destroying the eggs before the larvae hatch. Clean cultivation, including the destruction of spent leaves, is helpful, and spraying (according to local regulations) will also be necessary to kill off any eggs.

Aphids, when not too invasive, may be treated effectively with a blast from the hose. Otherwise use pyrethrum-based sprays or an insecticide spray containing carbaryl or malathion. Note a combination spray that covers both leaf spot and insects may be the best option.

Spuria irises are particularly susceptible to aphids, that hide right down among the leaves.

Tall Bearded rhizome affected by rot.

Sources

Buying tips

As with choosing any plant, it is wise to explore what varieties of iris will grow in your area before deciding which ones to buy. If possible visit an iris specialist nursery to see plants in bloom. Visit more than once so your purchases do not include only those that were blooming at one time. By purchasing plants that flower early, mid-season and late you can extend the bloom time considerably. Look for color, vigor, number of flower stalks, number of flowers and attractive, clean foliage.

When buying bearded irises it is usual to place an order for delivery after flowering has finished. This is because the new growth for next year's flowers takes place immediately after flowering and the rhizome that has just produced flowers is spent and will not produce again. If you purchase bearded irises or Siberians in pots, in flower, they are better planted out when the flower is finished, as there is often not room in the pot for expansion and new growth.

When purchasing Japanese or Louisianas you may be able to buy the plant in flower, in either a pot or growing bag. It can be left to grow in the pot (kept well-watered), or taken out and planted straight into your garden, provided it is watered assiduously until well-established in its new home.

Beautiful catalogs are available, but bear in mind that color accuracy of the flowers is hard to reproduce. Viewing the plants in flower gives you the opportunity to also note size, health, vigor and height. Many catalogs from iris specialists have only written descriptions; these are fine to purchase from, but remember that your mind-picture of "blue" may differ from that of the writer.

Border Bearded 'Lenora Pearl'

If you wish to exhibit your flowers, consider the timing of the particular show and purchase plants that will flower at the right time, and also in the colors or sections to be judged. For showing bearded irises, choose only plants that produce a candelabra display of flowers, i.e. well-spaced branches and flowers and lots of buds.

Aitken's Salmon Creek Garden
608 NW 119th Street
Vancouver, WA 98685
Tel (206) 573-4472
Website: www.flowerfantasy.net
*Extensive selection of all varieties, including Pacific
Coast hybrids and Dykes Medal-winner collection.
Ships to Canada.*

American Iris Society
Website: www.irises.org
*Twenty-four regions in the U.S., each with local
chapters. Many special interest groups, including
Pacific Coast Native, Siberian, Louisiana. Refer to
website for membership information and addresses.
Annual dues start at US$18.*

Anderson Iris Gardens
22179 Keather Avenue N
Forest Lake, MN 55025
Tel (612) 433-5268
Excellent variety of irises.

Argyle Acres
910 Pioneer Circle East
Argyle, TX 76226
Tel (940) 464-3680
Website: www.argyleacres.com
Historic and modern bearded irises.

Bayview Gardens
1201 Bay Street
Santa Cruz, CA 95060
Tel (831) 423-3656
*Beardless, bearded, hybrids, and many native
Pacific iris.*

George C. Bush, Clean Shaven Iris
1739 Memory Lane Extended
York, PA 17402
Tel (717) 755-0557
Siberian, Japanese, and some species iris.

Canadian Iris Society
Website: http://tor-pw1.netcom.ca/~cris/CIS.html
*Iris shows, sales and auctions, quarterly newsletter,
annual general meeting and various activities. Refer to*
*website for membership information and addresses.
Annual dues start at CA$10.*

Cooley's Gardens
11553 Silverton Road NE
PO Box 126
Silverton, OR 97381
Toll-Free Tel 1-800-225-5391
Tel (503) 873-5463; Fax (503) 873-5812
Website: www.cooleysgardens.com
Well-reputed nursery sells Tall Bearded iris.

Draycott Gardens
16815 Falls Road
Upperco, MD 21155
Tel (410) 374-4788
*Beardless iris – Siberian, Japanese, a few Louisiana
and species.*

Erin Mills Iris Garden
3070 Windwood Drive
Mississauga, ON L5N 2K3
Tel (905) 567-8545
Website: www.netcom/ca/~cris/erinmills
*All varieties of Ontario-climatized bearded and Siberian
iris. Canada only.*

Harmony Iris Gardens
PO Box 3731
Santa Rosa, CA 95402-3731
US Toll-Free Tel 1-888-600-5620
Tel (707) 585-1800; Fax (707) 523-0636
*Tall, Border, Intermediate, Miniature Tall, and
Standard Dwarf bearded, Louisiana, and Spuria irises.*

Historic Iris Preservation Society
Website: www.worldiris.com
*"To help preserve iris heritage by locating at-risk irises
and bringing them together with irisarians who want to
grow and perpetuate them." Refer to website for
membership information and addresses. Annual dues
start at US$5.*

Iris & Plus
595 River Street
Cowansville, PQ J2K 3G6
Tel/Fax (450) 266-0181

Website: www.irisplus.com
*More than 400 hardy bearded iris – germanica,
intermediate, dwarf, Japanese and Siberian. Ships to
USA.*

Iris City Gardens
7675 Younger Creek Road
Primm Springs, TN 38476
Toll-Free Tel 1-800-934-4747
Tel (615) 799-2179
*Beardless, Japanese, Louisiana, Siberian, species
crosses, water garden, and antique Tall Bearded irises.*

Keith Keppel
PO Box 18154
Salem, OR 97305
Tel (503) 391-9241
*Reputed grower of Tall Bearded and median irises.
Send US$2 for informative catalog.*

Long's Gardens
3240 Broadway, PO Box 19
Boulder, CO 80306
Tel (303) 442-2353
Tall Bearded, border, dwarf, median, and aril iris.

McMillen's Iris Garden
RR 1
Norwich, ON N0J 1P0
Tel (519) 468-6508; Fax (519) 468-3214
Website: www.execuline.com/~iris/
*Well-known for their beardeds and Siberians. Ships to
USA.*

Maryott's Iris Gardens
PO Box 1177
Freedom, CA 95019
Toll-Free Tel 1-877-937-4747
Tel (408) 722-1810; Fax (408) 722-2217
Website: www.irisgarden.com
Specialists in bearded iris, including re-blooming.

Nicholls Garden
4724 Angus Drive
Gainesville, VA 20155-1217
Tel (703) 754-9623

Website: www.nichollsgardens.com
*Siberian, Japanese, Louisiana, species and all varieties
of re-blooming beardeds.*

Parkside Gardens
251 Demetri Way
Salt Spring Island, BC V8K 1X3
*Large collection of hardy irises including Siberian,
Japanese, water irises and damp-land species irises.*

Redbud Lane Iris Garden
Route 1 Box 141
Kansas IL 61933
Tel (217) 948-5478
Great selection of beardless and other iris.

Schreiner's Gardens
3525 Quinaby Road NE
Salem, OR 97303
Toll-Free Tel 1-800-525-2367
Website: www.schreinersgardens.com
*Award-winning hybridizers of Tall Bearded iris offer
more than 400 varieties. Ships worldwide.*

Species Iris Group of North America
3 Wolters Street
Hickory Creek, TX 75065-3214
Website: www.signa.org
*Dedicated to the study of the wild species of the genus
Iris. Dues start at US$5.*

Sutton's Iris Garden
16592 Road 208
Porterville, CA 93257
Toll-Free Tel 1-888-558-5107
Fax (559) 784-6701
Website: www.suttoniris.com
*Tall Bearded, median and re-blooming irises. Ships to
Canada.*

Willow Bend Farm
1154 Hwy 65
Eckert, CO 81418
Tel (970) 835-3389
*Tall Bearded, smaller iris, Arilbreds, Dykes Medal-
winners.*

Glossary

Above: Japanese 'Shikinjo'
Opposite: Tall Bearded 'Color Magician'

Amoena	Bearded iris with white standards and colored falls.
Anthers	The male pollen-bearing part of the flower.
Apogon	A beardless, rhizomatous iris.
Beards	Peculiar to bearded irises, made up of colored filaments and found in the center of the top of the fall.
Bee pod	A seed pod resulting from bee pollination.
Bicolor	A color pattern; standards a lighter color, falls a different darker color.
Bi-tone	Two shades of the same color.
Bracts	Leaf-like structure enclosing the pods and also the branches.
Chromosome	The rod-like structures of the cell nucleus that carry the genes.
Colchicine	A naturally occurring plant chemical extracted from the fall crocus *Colchicum autumnale*, used in a process to treat a diploid iris and thus produce a tetraploid.
Cultivar	A variety of a plant produced by hybridization, distinguished from a botanical variety, or subdivision of a species.
Diploid	A plant cell with two complete sets of chromosomes.
Falls	The three lower petals of the flower.
Fan	Descriptive term for the leaf formation.
Genus	Taxonomic term used to include all the species in a group of plants.
Hafts	The narrow constricted part of the falls, or shoulders, often bearing distinct patterns.
Hybrid	Offspring of genetically unlike parents, e.g. from two species.
Increase	New rhizomes produced by any rhizome in a season. If separated from the mother plant these form individual new plants.
Luminata	Distinct color pattern of flower: the heart of the flower is without color and the outer parts of the flower have a smooth colored wash.
Natural hybrid	A hybrid resulting from pollination by natural forces, e.g. by insects.
Ovary	The female part of the flower that contains the ovules, or potential seeds.
Perianth	The standards and falls of the iris flower.
Perianth tube	The tubular connection between the ovary and the perianth sections.

Plicata	Distinct color pattern of flower: darker colored pattern over white or cream, appears in a dotted and stippled effect around the edge of the standards and falls.
Pogon	Bearded iris.
Remontancy	The ability to flower more than once in a season.
Rhizome	A swollen stem that stores nutrients and moisture enabling the plant to withstand dry periods.
Self	Flower of a single color.
Signal	Usually yellow marking located on the falls of beardless irises.
Socket	The term used to describe the area supporting the flower buds.
Spathe	A papery covering surrounding the base of the flower.
Stamen	Part of the flower supporting the male pollen-bearing anthers.
Standards	The three uppermost petals of the flower.
Stigma or Stigmatic lip	The receptive female part of the flower situated on the underside of the style arms.
Stippling	Dotted pattern.
Stolon	Horizontal stem used by the plant to extend through the soil and to reproduce.
Style	The extension of the ovary that bears the stigma.
Style arms	Three are situated in the heart of the flower, inside the standards.
Substance	Describes the quality of the petals and thus the ability of the flower to hold its shape.
Taxonomy	The naming and classification of living organisms.
Tetraploid	A cell having four sets of chromosomes.
Variegata	Bearded irises that have yellow standards and brown or red-brown falls.

Border Bearded 'Steeler Little'

Bibliography

Anley, Gwendolyn *Irises. Their Culture and Selection* W.H. & L. Collingridge Ltd., 1946

Caillet, Marie and Joseph K. Mertzweiller (Ed) *The Louisiana Iris* Texas Gardener Press, 1988

Glasgow, Karen *Irises for New Zealand Gardens* Godwit, 1996

Grosvenor, Graeme *Iris – Flower of the Rainbow* Kangaroo Press, 1997

McEwen, Currier *The Siberian Iris* Timber Press, Inc., 1996

— *The Japanese Iris* University Press of New England, 1990

Phillips, Roger and Rix, Martyn *Perennials* (Vol. 1) Pan Books Ltd., 1991

Shear, William *The Gardener's Iris Book* Taunton Press, 1998

Stebbings, Geoff *The Gardener's Guide to Growing Irises* Timber Press Inc., 1997

Stevens, Jean *The Iris and its Culture* Lothian Publishing Co. Pty. Ltd., 1952

Warburton/Hamblin *The World of Irises* American Iris Society, 1978.

Aitken's Salmon Creek Garden Catalogue, U.S.A.

American Iris Society Bulletin

Report of the 1st International Symposium on Iris, 1963 Tipografia Giuntina, Florence

New Zealand Iris Society Booklets

New Zealand Iris Society Bulletins

Schreiner's Catalogs, U.S.A.

Tempo Two Catalogs, Australia

Index